Penguin Books

AMAZING TRIVIA FROM THE WORLD OF BASEBALL

Stan Fischler is North America's most prolific author of sports books. His works include *The Comeback Yankees, Showdown — Baseball's Ultimate Confrontations* and *The Best, Worst and Most Unusual in Sports*. This marks his 60th book.

At age five Fischler saw his first live baseball game. The venue was Ebbets Field and when Dolph Camilli of the Brooklyn Dodgers walloped the ball over the right field fence and onto Bedford Avenue, Fischler became a diamond addict for life. He was there when the Brooklyns won their first World Series and has chronicled the rise of the Montreal Expos and Toronto Blue Jays in his weekly column, "Inside Sports," carried by *The Toronto Star* syndicate.

In more than 40 years of baseball-watching, Fischler has seen them all, from one-armed Pete Gray of the St. Louis Browns to Satchel Paige, pitching in the Negro National League. His favorite player of all time is Stan (The Man) Musial; his biggest thrill was watching the Browns win the pennant in 1944 and his most grievous disappointment occurred when Bobby Thomson hit that dreadful home run against Ralph Branca at the Polo Grounds in 1951. To this day Fischler maintains that it was foul.

Stan Fischler's AMAZING TRIVIA FROM THE WORLD OF BASEBALL

By STAN and SHIRLEY FISCHLER

COPY EDITOR
Roger Waltzman

RESEARCH EDITOR
David Lippman

Penguin Books

Penguin Books Ltd., Harmondsworth, Middlesex, England
Penguin Books Ltd., 40 West 23rd Street, New York, New York, 10010, U.S.A.
Penguin Books Australia Ltd., Ringwood, Victoria, Australia
Penguin Books Canada Ltd., 2801 John Street, Markham, Ontario, Canada L3R 1B4
Penguin Books (N.Z.) Ltd., 182-190 Wairau Road, Auckland 10, New Zealand

Published in 1984

Canadian Cataloguing in Publication Data

Fischler, Stan, 1932-
 Amazing trivia from the world of baseball

ISBN 0-14-007200-4

1. Baseball - Canada - Miscellanea. 2. Baseball -
United States — Miscellanea. I. Title.

GV867.3.F57 1984   796.357'02   C84-098138-4

Typeset by Jay Tee Graphics Ltd.
Manufactured in Canada

Cover photo: Miller Services

ACKNOWLEDGEMENTS

The authors would like to take this opportunity to thank those who have hidden behind the typewriters, archives, record books and yellowed newsclippings without whom this book would not have been possible. That their names are not in five-inch type does not in any way detract from the huge efforts. To the following, a standing ovation:

Bob Duff, Dave Ferry, Paul Tomizawa, Seth Popper, Marie Acampora, Debbie Klein, Bob Colasuonno, Doug Sutherland, Ken Juba, Bob Talmage, Dan Mahoney, Ken Albert, Stephen Nacco, Andrew Lippman, Jack Grasso, Jean-Louis Lalonde, Bob Stampleman and Renata Jacynicz.

ACKNOWLEDGMENTS

Who was the first man to homer into a snowbank?
In 1969, the Montreal Expos were forced to endure not
only a last-place season, but also a massive snow job in
September, when premature blizzards cancelled several
games.

Their luck did not improve in 1970, when six fleecy
inches fell on May 6th. The hard-pressed groundskeepers
managed to push the snow aside, but Rusty Staub became
the first man to homer into a snowbank.

His shot cleared the rightfield fence, sank into the snowbank, and disappeared.

• • •

**Al Downing gave up Henry Aaron's 715th home run.
What was Downing's uniform number?**
In supreme irony, Al Downing — the Yankees' first Black
pitcher in the early '60s — wore number 44 when he was
with the Los Angeles Dodgers and number 44 when he
gave up home run number 715 to Aaron in Atlanta, on
April 8th, 1974.

The irony? Another player was wearing 44 on that
historic occasion . . . Henry Aaron.

• • •

**An original Blue Jay set a Major League record. Do you
recall who the player was and what the record was?**
On November 5, 1976, the Toronto Blue Jays drafted their
first players. The first player picked came from the
Baltimore Orioles organization.

That player was Bob Bailor, and so far, he'd been no
more than a utility infielder. With the Jays, however, he
set a record by batting .310. It was the highest average by
a player on an expansion team in the first year of its existence.

He played a variety of positions for the Jays, including
the outfield and all infield positions except first base. On
three occasions, he was called in to pitch, showing

Toronto's desperation. As a pitcher, Bailor was a great out-fielder — his ERA was 9.00.

Bailor's offense fell noticeably from .264 in 1978 to .229 in 1979. In 1980 he hit .236 and was traded to the Mets.

• • •

Who was the shortest ball player to start an All-Star game?

Freddie Patek of the Kansas City Royals was named to start the 1978 All-Star Game for the American League in San Diego. Patek stood at 5 feet, 4 inches. A few years later, he would enjoy a two-home-run day, which put him past Phil Rizzuto on the list of home runs by short short-stops. Rizzuto had already passed Patek in height — he's 5 foot-6!

• • •

What did Warren Spahn do to post a 23-7 record . . . at age 42?

He switched from power pitching to finesse. Spahn was aware in 1963 that at age 42 he was past his prime, even though he had posted two no-hitters the previous two seasons. Thus, he evolved from strikeout ace to control pit-cher, conceding the middle 13 inches of home plate to the batter, but claiming the outside two inches for himself. He aimed his pitches for these spots, and won 23 games, not-ching a 2.60 ERA and seven shutouts for the Milwaukee Braves.

Yet it was the setting of Spahn's sun. He never had another winning season, although he toiled for San Fran-cisco and the Mets in an effort to win 373 games, which would tie him with Christy Mathewson as the National League leader. Spahn failed in his effort and ended with "only" 363.

• • •

How long was the longest game in baseball history?
On May 1, 1920, the Brooklyn Dodgers and the Boston
Braves squared off in what would become a 26-inning duel.
At the end of the 26th, with darkness coming on, the game
was called — a 1-1 tie. Now that's futility!

But what made it worse was that on the very next day
the Dodgers lost to the Phillies in 13 innings. After that,
the Bums lost again, to the Braves, in 19 innings. They
played 58 innings in three days and couldn't win a single
ball game.

The 1964 Mets might sympathize. They spent ten and a
half hours losing a doubleheader to the San Francisco
Giants on May 31. The two Met games were gruelling.

A crowd of 57,037 people turned out to watch 32 innings
of baseball — nine in the opener and 23 in the finale, with
nine hours and 52 minutes of playing time. There were 36
strikeouts in the opener and 47 for the doubleheader. Both
are records. The Mets pulled off the second triple play of
their short history, and Willie Mays played shortstop for
the second and last time in his career, as the Giants juggled players in an effort to win. At seven hours and 23
minutes, this second game was the longest (time) in major
league history.

That day also saw a young pitcher come in for the Giants
in the bottom of the fifteenth of the finale. The pitcher
quickly found himself in trouble and the Giants' catcher,
Tom Haller, told the youngster to use a spitball out of
sheer desperation. The pitcher did use his spitter and won
the game. He went on to win 300 more games. His name?
Gaylord Perry.

● ● ●

**This Toronto native was the pride of Flatbush when he
played for the Dodgers but he claims that manager Leo
Durocher ruined his career. Who was he?**
None other than Goodwin George (Goody) Rosen, who
came to Brooklyn in 1937 and finished his major league

career a decade later. Goody was his own biggest fan. He believed that his greatness was only limited by the outfield walls with which he was in constant conflict. In 1938, for example, he nearly killed himself crashing into a wall at Sportsmans Park in St. Louis. "With the ability I had," said Goody, "there's no telling how good I might have been if I hadn't run into the wall."

During Rosen's early years he was managed by the irascible Leo (The Lip) Durocher, who was as much a Brooklyn landmark as Ebbetts Field itself. Unfortunately for Goody, Durocher and Rosen did not always see eye to eye. "I used to fight with him all the time," said Rosen. "One year, I guess it was 1939, I'd been leading the league for the first month and a half. Now I tear up an ankle. Durocher comes to me crying that I'm the team leader and he needs me in there every day. So I continue to play on that bum ankle. My battin' average does a dive and I wind up gettin' sent down to Montreal."

The Canadian outfielder returned to the Dodgers in 1944 and enjoyed the most successful seasons of his life. In 1945 he nearly won the National League batting title when he hit .325. "I should have won it," Rosen insisted. "Tommy Holmes of the Braves and I were neck-and-neck most of the season. But I'm playin' centerfield between Dixie Walker and Augie Galan. Neither of them had any speed. They wore me out.

"We go into Philadelphia — worst team in the league. Seven games. That's where I should have picked up some ground. Instead of that, I only get five hits in thirty-three times at bat. Naw, it wasn't their pitching. I was makin' contact. Just kept hittin' the ball right at somebody."

Ironically, Rosen completed his major league career wearing the colors of the arch-enemy, the New York Giants. Goody claimed that Brooklyn boss Branch Rickey traded him in retaliation for a salary increase he demanded — and won.

"Actually," Goody recalled, "I started the 1946 season

with Brooklyn and everything seemed hunky-dory until we had a series with the Giants at their ball park, the Polo Grounds. I'm on my way up to the ball park on the subway when I pick up a paper. There's a headline: 'ROSEN SOLD TO THE GIANTS FOR $50,000 AND TWO PLAYERS.' That's how I find out I've been traded."

The Giants and Dodgers played a doubleheader that day and Rosen smote the ball all over the place. It was one of the best days he ever had and he won ovation after ovation from just about everyone except the man in the Dodgers' dugout, Leo Durocher.

•   •   •

When did a dead man score a run?
It was July 14, 1903 and the two teams from Benson and Willmar were playing a doubleheader in the blistering Minnesota heat. By the end of the first game the players were tired, so by the second they were really suffering from the heat. Then the second game went into extra innings and the players moaned with fatigue and frustration.

Thielman, the pitcher for Willmar, heaved himself up to the plate and sluggishly swung for a single. O'Toole was the next batter up and he hit the ball solidly, sending it into the outfield. As best he could, Thielman slowed down and began to run the bases as O'Toole headed for first. Halfway between second and third, Thielman slowed down again and began to lose his balance, eventually collapsing onto the sack at third. As O'Toole came around from second he wasn't sure what to do, since he knew that he couldn't pass a runner ahead of him. Instead, he picked up Thielman, slung him across his shoulder and carried him. Upon reaching home plate, O'Toole lowered Thielman's foot to touch the base and then touched it himself just as the ball reached the catcher's mitt.

O'Toole had directly assisted in the scoring of two runs and his fellow players gathered around to congratulate him. Out from the stands emerged a doctor who examined Thielman, who was lying on the ground.

"This man died back there on third base. His heart broke down under the strain," the doctor said.

And so a run was scored by a dead man — an occurrence in baseball history that must be labeled "unique."

• • •

The Tinker-to-Evers-to-Chance double-play combination was one of baseball's greatest. Yet few realize that for years Tinker and Evers refused to talk to each other. What was the cause of the feud?

It started because of a misunderstanding they had one day in 1909 in Bedford, Indiana, where they were to play an exhibition game. The Cubs, who were staying at a local hotel, would dress in their rooms and then take a taxi to the ball park.

On this day Evers dressed before any of his teammates, walked down to the front of the hotel and hailed a cab. A few minutes later his teammates reached the street but could not find a hack. When the hack that had taken Evers to the ball park returned, some of them climbed in and took off.

Tinker, apparently, was dismayed that Evers took off without him and confronted him in the dressing room. "Who do you think you are, riding all by yourself?" he demanded.

Evers responded in kind and in a trice they were slugging away. Teammates eventually pried them apart but they were not through with each other. "If you ever talk to me again," snapped Tinker, "there'll be another fight. Don't talk to me, and I won't talk to you."

Evers agreed and from that moment on the vow of silence was scrupulously maintained. Ironically, it was that disagreement and the ensuing agreement that made them a devastating combination, according to baseball historian Frank G. Menke.

12

"The combination became great really because of that feud," said Menke. "Whenever Evers got the ball and Tinker was to take the throw, Evers would fire it at him with all his power, even if he was only ten feet away. Tinker did the same, with the result that the plays at second were of chain-lightning variety and enabled the non-speaking pair — together with Frank Chance — to create an immortal double-play combination."

● ● ●

Canada was home to one of the most unusual players of all time, a one-armed outfielder. Who was he and where did he play?

His real name was Peter J. Wyshner and he was born in Nanticoke, Pennsylvania, a scruffy coal-mining town near Wilkes-Barre. In later years he would be known as Peter Gray, a one-armed player who actually became a regular in the major leagues with the St. Louis Browns.

When he was six years old Pete hopped a farmer's provision wagon, fell off, and caught his right arm in the spokes. The arm was mangled, and had to be amputated above the elbow. The handicap never hampered Pete's enthusiasm for sports. He continued to play baseball, learning to bat from the left side with one hand. "He had a superb batting eye and was a fast runner," wrote William B. Mead, an author with a keen interest in Gray. "Gray mixed line drives with well-executed bunts, some down the third-base line, others dragged past the pitcher."

Batting was less of a problem for the one-armed Gray than fielding. As an outfielder, he had to solve the puzzle of trapping the ball in his glove but then getting the glove off so that he could toss the ball back in play. With only one arm, Gray had to catch the ball with a glove on and throw it with the glove off.

"He managed this cleverly and deftly," said Mead. "Removing almost all the padding from his glove, Gray wore it on his fingertips with his little finger out. He would catch the ball, stick his glove under the stump of his right arm, draw the ball clear with his left hand, and throw it to the infield."

After starring for semi-pro teams, Gray felt he was ready for the professional ranks but he couldn't get a break in the United States. Pro teams simply would not grant a try-out to a player with only one arm. It was then that he found a haven in Canada. He played in Three Rivers, Quebec, before returning to the States where he hooked on with the country's best semi-pro team, the Brooklyn Bush-wicks, although not before he convinced a skeptical owner, Max Rosner, that he could play. Gray handed Rosner a ten-dollar bill. "Take this and keep it if I don't make good," Gray said. And Gray did make good.

When Three Rivers was admitted to the Canadian-American League in 1942, Gray rejoined his old club and it was with the Canadian team that he made his first impact on the national scene. Despite injuries, Gray bat-ted .381 and won himself a tryout with the Toronto Maple Leafs of the International League in 1943.

Some observers believed that Gray was certainly good enough to make the Toronto club but that he had argued with manager Burleigh Grimes and was cut without being given a fair chance. After returning home, Gray was sum-moned by the Memphis Chicks of the Class A Southern Association. He batted .299 in 1943 and was a sensation, although still not considered good enough for the majors. A year later he hit .333 for Memphis, stole 63 bases and led the Southern Association in fielding percentage. He was also voted the league's most valuable player.

Now there was no keeping him out of the big leagues and, sure enough, the St. Louis Browns bought Gray for $20,000. The St. Louis club was the defending American League champion and promised to be a contender again in 1945. But once Browns manager Luke Sewell had a chance to see Gray at spring training he suffered grave doubts. "When I got him," said Sewell, "I knew he couldn't make it. He didn't belong in the majors and he knew he was being exploited. When he got up to the majors the infielders just came right in on him, and he couldn't get on with those bunts and drags that he used in the minors. He had no power. Pete just couldn't play major league ball."

Gray played 77 games for the Browns in 1945 and was sent up to pinch-hit a dozen times. He batted .218 with six doubles and two triples. He stole five bases. But Gray suffered in the outfield because of his disability, and his teammates knew it.

"There were an awful lot of ground balls hit to center field," said Mark Christman, a star of that St. Louis team. "When the kids who hit those balls were pretty good runners, they could keep on going and wind up at second base. I know that cost us eight or ten ball games."

Gray was demoted to Toledo the following season and bounced around the minors until 1949, when he completed his baseball career with Dallas. Looking back at his one season in the American League sun, Gray once observed: "I knew I couldn't stay up too long. I didn't have the power. It seemed I hit a lot of line drives that they'd catch ten or fifteen feet from the fence. Just not quite far enough."

But he did make a living playing baseball, and the people who saw him in Three Rivers, St. Louis and Memphis will never forget Pete Gray.

• • •

When was the first night game in World Series history?
The first night game (October 13, 1971) was the fourth game of the 1971 classic between the Baltimore Orioles and the Pittsburgh Pirates. This event brought an end to the weekday World Series game.

The Orioles knocked starter Luke Walker out of the box in the first inning, scoring three runs. Bruce Kison came in to relieve and pitched one-hit ball over 6 1/3 innings.

Meanwhile the Pirates came back to tie the score, and

finally won the game on a pinch-hit single, making them the first team to win a World Series night game.

● ● ●

Belleville, Ontario was the birthplace of a doctor's son who seemed to have a glorious career before him. Yet the highlight of his Major League life was one inning of a World Series game. Name that righthander.
Johnny Rutherford appeared to be a star in the Brooklyn Dodgers firmament when he was summoned to the majors in 1952. He had a 7-7 record and a 4.25 earned run average. In the bitter World Series between the Dodgers and New York Yankees, Rutherford pitched one inning of the fourth game and gave up one run on one hit as Allie Reynolds of the Yankees pitched a 2-0 shutout.

Prior to his series appearance Rutherford impressed with a two-hitter in August 1952, beating the St. Louis Cardinals, 3-1. In all he pitched 11 games in relief and 11 starts but never saw the bigs again after his stint against the Yankees.

● ● ●

How did the Boston Braves' bleachers get the name "Jury Box"?
In Braves' Field, to the side nearest the tracks of the Boston and Main Railroad, there was a bleacher section in which the most diehard fans would sit. One afternoon, the section was occupied by exactly 12 fans. A Boston writer counted them and wrote that their verdict was "guilty." Henceforth, the section was called the "Jury Box," and became legend.

● ● ●

One of the National Leagues original rules would be of great use to modern umpires. What was it?
One of the original rules of the National League, written in 1876, read: "Should the umpire be unable to see

whether a catch has been fairly made or not, he shall be at liberty to appeal to the bystanders, and to render his decision according to the fairest testimony at hand."

Can you imagine the kind of "testimony" one of today's umps would get?

* * *

The ball Hank Aaron hit for his record-breaking 715th home run was unusual . . . Do you know in what way?
As Hank Aaron neared career home run 715, the Braves worried about hordes of people running up waving "home run ball 715" and demanding rewards. Consequently the National League began to stamp the date and the number 715 in invisible ink on balls that were used only when Aaron came to bat.

In 1973, San Francisco Giant pitcher Juan Marichal observed all of the hullabaloo around Aaron's arrival at bat — umpires reaching into special pouches and calling for balls — and got very nervous. Unaware of the importance of the ball, Juan said he was afraid that the one he got from the ump would split in two and emit smoke as he tried his screwball!

* * *

Which Expo hit the first grand slam in the team's history?
Mack (The Knife) Jones was the hitter, and he did it on May 10, 1969, against the Cincinnati Reds in Montreal.

The victim was Jack Fisher, who was at the terminus of his career. Fisher had given up two other famous homers — Ted Williams' final shot, in 1960, and Roger Maris's 60th in 1961. Fisher also had the dubious honor of leading the National League in games lost by a pitcher in 1965. As a New York Met, he won 8 — and lost 24.

* * *

1

1. The number 56 has special significance to Joe DiMaggio's hitting streak, other than the number of games in which he safely hit. What is it?
2. Why must all pitching records prior to 1893 be viewed differently from those kept after that year?
3. How many balls constituted a walk in these years? 1887, 1885, 1884, 1881, 1880, 1879?
4. What makes stolen base records between 1886-1898 unusual?
5. In 1887, 11 players hit .400 or better. What unusual factor helped their averages?
6. In the modern era (post 1900), what is a pitcher's record for the most wins in a single season?
7. Name the first players to hit (A) 30 (B) 40 (C) 50 and (D) 60 homeruns?
8. If Henry Chadwick was called "The Father of Baseball," what was Alexander Cartwright called?
9. How many stitches are there on a baseball?
10. Six different men have won the MVP award three times. Name them.

Answers begin on page 172.

A pitcher was once knocked down by a bolt of lightning! Who was the unfortunate fellow?

Ray Caldwell of Cleveland had a 2-1 lead against the Philadelphia A's in the top of the ninth on August 8, 1919. After retiring the first two batters, the skies darkened, and a bolt of lightning hit Caldwell, knocking him down.

When he picked himself up, miraculously unharmed, Ray quickly finished off the last batter, terrified that lightning might strike twice in the same place!

Caldwell was not the only victim of lightning in baseball. Once the Washington Senators attained a lead in the early innings of a game. Manager Joe Cantillon, ecstatic over what appeared to be the imminent end of his team's 18-game losing streak, began to celebrate.

Instead, torrential rains came and washed out the potential victory. The pathetic Senators fled to their horse-drawn bus. As the last man boarded, a lightning bolt struck and killed the two horses.

Cantillon looked at his players, raised his hands skyward and said, "What kind of justice is there in heaven that strikes those poor creatures dead and leaves these miserable vegetables sitting in here alive?"

Lightning once helped Gavvy Cravath of the Phillies hit a home run against the Giants to win a game. During a scoreless tie, a thunderstorm came in from the west, blackening the skies. As Red Ames of the Giants delivered a pitch to Cravath, lightning illuminated it. Cravath hit it deep to the outfield, as the crowd fell silent. Then everyone in the park heard the ball rattle the wooden bleachers for the only run of the game.

• • •

When did baseball's first night game take place?

On May 24, 1935, the Cincinnati Reds defeated the Philadelphia Phillies, 2-1, in the majors' first night game. President Franklin D. Roosevelt turned on the $50,000 lights from the White House with a special remote switch, for the benefit of the 20,422 spectators.

The idea of night baseball was conceived by Larry Mac-Phail, the Reds' General Manager, and it was almost universally attacked at first. Washington owner Clark Griffith said, "There is no chance of night baseball ever becoming popular in the bigger cities. People there are educated to see the best there is, and will stand only for the best. High-class baseball cannot be played under artificial light."

Today the Texas Rangers play all their home games at night, and most World Series games are played at night.

• • •

Bob Lemon once blew a 10-0 lead! How did this happen?

In 1950 Bob Lemon of the Cleveland Indians led the American League with 23 wins, but he missed a chance for his 24th. On August 28, leading the game by a whopping 10-0, Lemon incredibly lost all of his control, gave up 15 runs and lost to the Red Sox, 15-14. Talk about fear of success!

• • •

Joe Cronin had an unusual entry to Major League baseball. Do you remember the circumstances surrounding the Hall-of-Famer's arrival on the American League scene?

Washington Senator scout Joe Engel could never explain why he bought Joe Cronin for the Senators from Kansas City. Cronin's fielding was erratic and he was hitting about .220 for K.C.

While Engel was sitting in the telegraph office in Kansas City, sending the wire to Senator owner Clark Griffith, he realized that Griffith would be furious over the price tag on Cronin.

So the scout wrote a letter to Griffith's adopted daughter,

whom he kidded a lot, telling her that he was "bringing (her) a young sweetie."

Eventually, Engel reached Washington with Cronin in tow. When he found Mildred Griffith, he boomed at her, "Hello, Mildred, I've brought you a husband. Meet Joe Cronin."

Boy and girl stared at each other in embarrassed silence. Griffith was furious anyway, but Senator manager Bucky Harris saw that Cronin had talent, and Harris played Cronin, benching regular Bobby Reeves.

Griffith, still annoyed, sent Harris a wire while the Senators were on a road trip: "Reeves will never become great if you don't use him more."

Harris snapped back, "Neither will Cronin."

Ultimately, Cronin became the outstanding shortstop of his day — and he lived up to Engel's announcement: he married Mildred, and they lived happily ever after.

• • •

Name the current National Hockey League manager who once starred on the diamond in Canadian professional baseball.

Emile (The Cat) Francis, president and general manager of the Hartford Whalers, starred for a number of western Canadian teams during the early 1950s. Francis, who played goal for the Chicago Black Hawks and New York Rangers, was an accomplished shortstop who later took to both managing and playing.

One of his more power-packed teams was the North Battleford (Saskatchewan) Beavers from Francis' home town. It was a club loaded with black players, many of whom made their way to the American and National League.

"We played in the old Western Canada League," Francis recalls. "Later its name was changed to the Canadian-American League. In any case we had some of the best players on the continent. One year no less than 26 were signed out of our league into the majors."

Such accomplished major leaguers as Don Buford, Ron Fairly and Tom Haller played for and against Francis, not to mention a number of superb college stars. "They couldn't play professional ball in the States," Francis remembers, "so they'd come up to Canada, get paid and get good experience. Nobody snitched on them either."

A spunky hockey player, Francis was no less pugnacious on the diamond. He was involved in a number of bristling episodes, including one game that erupted into a full-scale riot. It took place in Rosetown, Saskatchewan, during a tournament involving teams from the United States and Cuba.

"We were playing this team — the Indian Head Cubans — and the stakes were high," says Francis. "It was something like $2,000 per man and nobody wanted to lose.

"Well on this one play one of our players slid hard into second and upset the Cuban shortstop. Next thing we know the whole bunch of the Cubans run off the field and I was damned if I could figure out what they were up to; but it didn't take long for me to understand. They had gone to the bat rack and they were coming back at us with bats.

"The battle that followed took an hour and a half to cool down but that wasn't the half of it. Two of the Cubans took of after one of our players. I could see them chase him out to the parking lot and I followed as they went down a dirt road, heading for a farmer's house. My player was still in the lead and he made it to this farmhouse. He ran in, grabbed a butcher knife from the kitchen and came right out at the Cubans. They were all about to go at it — meanwhile, I pulled up a bad last — when just in time the Royal Canadian Mounted Police arrived and broke it up."

By the time the dust had cleared the game was resumed and Francis' team won. He got his knife-wielding player out of jail and headed for Moose Jaw for another game.

This time the knife-wielder came up with a perfect night, five hits in five times at bat.

"After the game," says Francis, "I got a wire from the local sports editor. He wrote: 'OUT OF THE FIVE HITS YOUR MAN GOT, HOW MANY CUBANS WERE SENT TO THE HOSPITAL?' "

Francis also teamed up on the baseball field with hockey Hall of Famers Max and Doug Bentley of Delisle, Saskatchewan, as well as other Bentley brothers.

"At one time I was surrounded by Bentleys. There were five altogether on my teams. One day a fan shouted at me: 'Francis, there's only one way you could've made this team; you must have married a Bentley'."

* * *

The famous "pine-tar" game of 1983 was finally concluded with a highly unusual switch in players' positions. Why did this happen?

When George Brett lashed his home run off Rich Gossage, putting the Royals ahead in the game, Jerry Mumphrey was out in center field for the Yankees.

The bat and the homer were called back for irregular use of pine-tar and the game was suspended, unleashing the now-famous "Tar Wars." Ultimately the American League president, Lee MacPhail, begrudgingly backed the umpires' ruling and the game was rescheduled to be completed. In the meantime over a month had passed and Jerry Mumphrey had been traded by the Yanks to the Houston Astros for Omar Moreno.

When the game resumed the Yankees had to substitute for Mumphrey, who was scheduled to bat in the bottom half of the ninth inning. Someone had to cover center field for the Royals' final two outs.

In order not to waste a pinch hitter, manager Billy Martin decided to send pitcher Ron Guidry, a fine overall athlete, to center field. Guidry didn't record any putouts or assists, and when he was scheduled to come up in the ninth, Martin substituted Oscar Gamble to pinch hit.

It was not the first time Ron Guidry had played the outfield. In 1979, he played the final out of the season in center, so the fans could see him one last time before winter.

• • •

Name the only man to amass over 3,000 hits without ever winning a batting title.
Considered one of the most intelligent men ever to play baseball, Eddie Collins combined physical agility and Ivy League academic brilliance to achieve a 25-year career — with the Philadelphia A's and the Chicago White Sox.

Collins played second base from 1906 to 1926, first with Connie Mack's Philadelphia A's. There, he spearheaded a team which won four pennants in five years. In 1915 he was traded to the Chicago White Sox, but Collins alertly made sure that his high-paying A's contract followed him to Chicago. White Sox owner Charlie Comiskey was well known for habitually underpaying his players.

When gamblers approached the White Sox players in 1919 to con them into throwing the series (for which they became known as the "Black Sox"), they didn't even try to speak to the scrupulously honest Collins. Then in the 1920s he returned to Philadelphia, and from 1927 to 1930, he was the team's primary pinch-hitter.

Along the way, Collins stole 743 bases, hit over .360 three times, including a high of .369 in 1920. His lifetime batting average was .333. Collins also notched 3,313 base hits. But he never won a batting title, unlike all the other men with 3,000 hits. You see, Collins was in the same league, at the same time, as Ty Cobb . . .

• • •

The National League's stolen bases leader in 1982 was a member of the Montreal Expos. Guess who?

24

The pride of Sanford, Florida, Tim Raines produced 78 stolen bases during the 1982 season. He also scored 90 runs, drove in 43 and batted .277.

• • •

Who hit the longest single in baseball history?

In 1974 Mike Schmidt of the Philadelphia Phillies hit a titanic shot in the Houston Astrodome that seemed destined not only to be a homer, but also to hit the roof of the cavernous covered stadium.

But as the ball went up it hit a loudspeaker hanging from the top of the stadium, and the ball plummeted back to earth. Schmidt had to settle for a single.

Schmidt wasn't the only player to have problems with Houston's Dome. When it was first built, the roof was glass. On May 23, 1965, the inevitable happened.

Astro centerfielder Jim Wynn, searching for a fly ball hit by the Giants' Jim Ray Hart, froze, blinded by the Texas sunlight streaming through the skylights and reflecting off the overhead beams. As Wynn stodd, transfixed, the ball landed behind him. Three runs scored, and the Giants won, 5-2.

The next day a squad of workmen armed with paint guns sprayed over the skylights. Then the outfield grass, bereft of sunlight, yellowed and withered. The Astros tried resodding and painting the grass, before they bowed to the future. Finally, in 1966, the Dome unveiled the green plastic carpeting that would be known forever as AstroTurf.

• • •

How many players can you identify from the following nicknames?

1. The Bambino
2. The Man of a Thousand Curves
3. The Iron Man
4. Arky
5. Dizzy
6. The Scooter
7. The Fordham Flash

8. The Antelope
9. The Wild Horse of Osage
10. The Georgia Peach
11. Fireball
12. Yogi
13. The Big Train
14. Three-fingered Brown
15. Birdie
16. Kiki
17. Ducky-Wucky
18. The Flying Dutchman
19. Spider
20. Pee Wee
21. The Rajah
22. Preacher
23. Larrupin' Lou
24. Rapid Robert
25. Bobo
26. Old Reliable
27. The Lip .
28. Wahoo Sam
29. Push-'em-up Tony
30. Pie
31. The Grey Eagle
32. Pistol Pete
33. Little Napoleon
34. Harry the Horse
35. Black Mike
36. Goose
37. Big Poison
38. Little Poison
39. High Pockets
40. The Rabbit
41. Puddin' Head

42. The Whip
43. Big Six
44. King Kong
45. Peanuts
46. Schoolboy
47. Daffy
48. Mealticket
49. Stan the Man
50. Stubby
51. The Yankee Clipper
52. Jeep
53. Dazzy
54. Slats
55. The Sultan of Swat
56. Old Pete
57. The Duke of Tralee
58. The Old Fox
59. Gettysburg
60. The Crab
61. Arthur the Great
62. Frenchy
63. Flash
64. Smoky Joe
65. Butch
66. Cookie
67. Irish
68. Jigger
69. Dixie
70. The Cat
71. Wee Willie
72. Big Ed
73. Happy Jack
74. Satchel
75. Turkey Mike
76. Bullet Joe
77. The Miracle Man

78. Billy the Kid
79. Goofy
80. Jumpin' Joe
81. King Carl
82. Mr. Right Field
83. The Peerless Leader
84. Jughandle
85. Hawk
86. Country
87. Mule
88. Camera Eye
89. The Little Professor
90. Casey
91. Beauty
92. The Arkansas Traveler
93. The Old Roman
94. Memphis Bill
95. Pants
96. Ozark Ike
97. The Mad Russian
98. 'Oom Paul
99. Duster
100. Wildfire

(ANSWERS TO NICKNAME QUESTION)

1. George Herman "Babe" Ruth
2. John F. Sain
3. Joe McGinnity
4. Floyd Vaughan
5. Jerome Dean
6. Phil Rizzuto
7. Frank Frisch
8. Emil Verban
9. Pepper Martin
10. Ty Cobb
11. Virgil Trucks
12. Lawrence Berra
13. Walter Johnson
14. Mordecai Brown
15. George Tibbetts
16. Hazen Cuyler
17. Joe Medwick
18. John Peter (Honus) Wagner
19. John Jorgensen
20. Harold H. Reese
21. Rogers Hornsby
22. Elwood Roe
23. Lou Gehrig
24. Bob Feller
25. Louis Newsom
26. Tommy Henrich
27. Leo Durocher
28. Sam Crawford
29. Tony Lazzeri
30. Harold Traynor
31. Tris Speaker
32. Pete Reiser
33. John McGraw
34. Harry Heilmann
35. Mickey Cochrane
36. Leon Goslin and Rich Gossage
37. Paul Waner
38. Lloyd Waner
39. George Kelly

40. Walter J. Maranville	71. William H. Keeler
41. William Jones	72. Edward A. Walsh
42. Ewell Blackwell	73. John D. Chesbro
43. Christy Mathewson	74. Leroy Paige
44. Charles Keller and Dave Kingman	75. Michael Donlin
	76. Joe Bush
45. Harry Lowery	77. George Stallings
46. Lynwood T. Rowe	78. Billy Southworth
47. Paul Dean	79. Vernon Gomez
48. Carl Hubbell	80. Joe Dugan
49. Stan Musial	81. Carl Hubbell
50. Frank Overmire	82. Melvin Ott
51. Joe DiMaggio	83. Frank Chance
52. Lee Handley	84. Johnny Morrison
53. Arthur Vance	85. Ken Harrelson and Andre Dawson
54. Marty Marion	
55. George Herman Ruth	86. Enos Slaughter
	87. George Haas and Don Mueller
56. Grover Cleveland Alexander	
	88. Max Bishop
57. Roger Bresnahan	89. Dom DiMaggio
58. Clark Griffith	90. Charles Stengel
59. Eddie Plank	91. Dave Bancroft
60. Johnny Evers	92. Travis Jackson
61. Arthur Shires	93. Charles A. Comiskey
62. Stanley Bordagaray	
63. Joe Gordon	94. William Terry
64. Joe Wood	95. Clarence Rowland
65. Walter J. Henline	96. Gus Zernial
66. Harry A. Lavagetto	97. Lou Novikoff
67. Emil Meusel	98. Paul Derringer and Otto Krueger
68. Arnold Statz	
69. Fred Walker	99. Walter Mails
70. Harry Brecheen	100. Frank Schulte

• • •

George Gibson is regarded as one of the best managers in Pittsburgh Pirates' history and one of the best catchers as well. Can you name his Canadian home town?

Nicknamed "Moon," Gibson hailed from London, Ontario. He broke into the majors with Pittsburgh in 1905 and remained a big-leaguer until 1918. He later was hailed as one of the diamond game's most accomplished managers, leading the Cubs and the Pirates.

• • •

A Canadian, playing shortstop for a Major League team in Providence, introduced the glove to baseball. Who was he?

Arthur Irwin of Toronto had broken the third and fourth fingers of his left hand while playing for Providence in 1883. In those days teams carried ten or eleven players. Every man was his own substitute, playing as long as was physically possible. Determined to remain in the Providence lineup, Irwin visited a glovemaker in the city who took a buckskin driving glove and added some padding. He then sewed together the third and fourth fingers and presented the finished product to the shortstop.

When Irwin returned to the playing field the next day he expected to be ridiculed by players and fans alike, since a glove was unheard of and, besides, players were considered too manly to dare wear any protective material.

To his amazement, Irwin was not ridiculed and completed the game without a problem. Not long afterward another ball player who had not been injured, John Montgomery Ward, took a liking to Irwin's idea and ordered a glove. Nobody complained and soon hundreds of gloves were being ordered by enthusiastic ball players.

• • •

Can you recall the manager who was the first to manage his team from the bench and use a relief pitcher?

The manager was John J. McGraw, who took over the New York Giants in 1902, and didn't leave them until he retired in 1932. Among his pupils in baseball were Christy Mathewson, Frankie Frisch, Mel Ott, Bill Terry, Carl Hubbell and Casey Stengel.

The first relief pitcher was one of McGraw's ideas, too. Otis Crandall was sent to the pen in 1909, and he won seven games from there in 1910, and seven more in 1911, leading the National League both times. He became known as "Doc" Crandall, the physician who could heal broken ball games.

•　•　•

Can you recall the first player to hit 30 homers and steal 30 bases in a single season?
Willie Mays of the New York and San Francisco Giants did it in 1954 and 1965. He stole over 200 bases and hit 660 homers.

•　•　•

Which team compiled the longest consecutive winning streak in baseball history?
John J. McGraw's New York Giants won 26 consecutive games from September 7 to September 30, 1916. McGraw was an extremely tough loser and vowed not to finish in last place, as the team had the previous season.

At the start of the 1916 season, he cut from his roster such greats as Rube Marquard, Larry Doyle, Fred Merkle and Chief Meyers. By mid-season, the team had a different look, built around Slim Sallee, Ferdie Schupp, Pol Perritt and Jeff Tesreau, as well as home run champ Dave Robertson.

On September 7, the Giants defeated the contending Brooklyn Dodgers. The next day, they played a doubleheader with Philadelphia. Although Giant starter Pol Perritt won the opener, he became upset over the needling he had received from the Philadelphia players and begged

McGraw to let him pitch the nightcap. McGraw agreed, and Perritt pitched a four-hit shutout. The game so inspired the Giants that they rallied to win the next twenty-three straight.

Ironically, they finished fourth to the Brooklyn Dodgers, who won the pennant with the help of McGraw's castoffs . . . Rube Marquard, Chief Meyers, and Fred Merkle!

• • •

When was the first All-Star game played?
Not in 1933, the year that is often cited.

In 1911, Cleveland Indian star pitcher Addie Joss, a future Hall-of-Famer, died of tubercular meningitis. Joss had a 1.88 lifetime earned run average, second on the all-time list, and was a four-time 20-game winner.

To lessen the family's loss, a group of American League stars played the Cleveland Indians on July 24, 1911, in a benefit game for Joss's family. The All-Stars, led by Ty Cobb, Eddie Collins, Tris Speaker and Walter Johnson, won, 5-3, defeating such great Indians as Cy Young, Joe Jackson and Napoleon Lajoie.

• • •

John J. McGraw once fined a pitcher when he did an endorsement! How did this happen?
John McGraw fined pitcher Zeke Barnes when the pitcher reported with a bad ankle — sustained in a bathtub fall. He had been posing for an ad for bathmats, and slipped during the shooting.

• • •

White Sox pitcher George Medich has made some truly outstanding saves . . . but not on the field. Do you know how?
George Medich, nicknamed "Doc," is a qualified surgeon, affiliated with a hospital in Pittsburgh, Pennsylvania.

On at least two occasions, he saved the lives of fans,

when they were injured at the ballpark, while Medich was there with his team (but not actually pitching).

Medich is not the first ballplayer to start a career in medicine. Former relief pitcher Ron Taylor, a Canadian, after being an electrical engineer and pitcher, entered the medical field.

Taylor, a Toronto native, became the first major leaguer to return to the game as team physician when he became the Toronto Blue Jays' team doctor in February, 1979.

Taylor pitched for 11 years with five different clubs, including the 1969 World Champion Mets. He amassed 72 saves, a 45-43 record, and a 3.93 ERA. He received his medical and engineering degrees at the University of Toronto.

Another ballplayer-turned-doctor was Bobby Brown, a third baseman with the Yankees in the late forties and early fifties.

• • •

A new Major Leaguer once asked his coach "Where'll I hit it?" and hit the ball exactly in the direction that the coach suggested. Who was he?

When Branch Rickey, the Michigan baseball coach, was hired to manage the St. Louis Browns, he contacted a Michigan southpaw, George Sisler, who once fanned 20 out of 21 batters in a game, and asked him to come to St. Louis for a major league tryout.

In his first time at bat, Sisler turned to Rickey and asked him "Where'll I hit it, coach?" There were two men on base and young Sisler wasn't quite sure what he should do. Manager Rickey just grinned and responded, "Try the right-field fence, son." Needless to say, that's where the ball went, over the fence.

It's almost uncanny how good a hitter this pitcher was. He hit over .400 twice, and in 1920 got 257 hits in a single season. This is still a Major League record. In 1922, he hit

.420, tying the mark set by Ty Cobb. He was the MVP that year.

Sisler was the Hall of Fame's first first-baseman. And he even pitched 24 games, winning 5 and losing 6, over 15 years, with a 2.35 ERA.

On August 29, 1915, Sisler pitched against Walter Johnson in Washington. Sisler idolized Johnson, and, the night before the game, was unable to eat or sleep. Amazingly, he beat Johnson, 2-1, both pitchers getting hits.

After the game ended, Sisler recalls, "I thought maybe I'd go over and shake his hand and tell him that I was sorry I beat him, but I guess that was just the silly idea of a kid who had just come face to face with his idol and beaten him."

• • •

Who hit the first grand slam off Expo pitching?
On April 14, 1969, Dal Maxvill of the St. Louis Cardinals hit a grand slam off Larry Jaster, in Montreal's Jarry Park — the first the Expos allowed.

Jaster gave up one more to Maury Wills of the Dodgers before the year ended. Jaster didn't fare well in Montreal. He had a 1-6 record and a 5.49 ERA. The Expos shipped him to Atlanta in 1970.

The slam was one of Maxvill's paltry two homers for 1969. He hit .175 that year as the regular shortstop for the Cards. It just wasn't Jaster's day.

• • •

While playing for one of the worst teams in history, a Toronto-born pitcher produced a no-hitter. Who was he?
Richard John (Dick) Fowler became a member of the Philadelphia Athletics in 1941 and pitched commendably for two years before entering the Canadian armed forces. He returned from active duty in 1945 and rejoined the Athletics, one of the worst clubs known to man. Fowler's record was 1-2 but that winner was a no-hitter against the

St. Louis Browns. Fowler's last season was 1952, all spent with the pathetic A's. Nevertheless, he compiled a 66-79 record, which, under the circumstances, should have won him nomination for the Hall of Fame.

• • •

One of Fowler's teammates on the Athletics, also a Canadian, in 1942 produced an astonishing 17-14 record. Who was he and what was his wartime claim to fame?

Following the 1942 season, Philip (Babe) Marchildon, a native of Penetanguishene, Ontario, joined the Royal Canadian Air Force. A tail gunner, Marchildon was shot down with his bomber while laying mines off the coast of Denmark. Of seven crewmen, Marchildon was one of two survivors. He spent a year in a Nazi prisoner-of-war camp and lost thirty pounds.

Despite his wartime experience, Marchildon returned to the Athletics in June 1945 — but he was too weak to pitch. Nevertheless, club owner Connie Mack persuaded him to make one appearance for the team and Marchildon agreed. At the time the A's were drawing about 3,000 fans per game and Mack understood that an appearance by Marchildon would do wonders for the gate. He was right. More than 34,000 fans turned out for "Marchildon Night" and Phil obliged by pitching three innings, losing the game. He was given a $1,000 war bond for his stint. Mack kept the rest of the profits. A year later Marchildon was back in top form.

• • •

One player in World Series history was almost put on the disabled list by his owner after committing two costly errors in one game. Who were the protagonists in this bizarre drama, and when did it take place?

After making two miscues in the twelfth inning of the second game of the 1973 World Series, Mike Andrews was the wearer of goat horns as the Oakland A's and New York Mets tied the series at one game apiece.

Not that Andrews should really have been out there at second — after eight years in the majors, back injuries were taking their toll on him, and the A's had picked him up from the White Sox at the very end of the season as insurance. Second base was traditionally a hole for the A's.

Next day Charlie O. Finley, the A's active, outspoken owner, tried to put Andrews on the disabled list and have him replaced by Manny Trillo, a rookie at the time. Finley had Andrews examined by a doctor, who issued a statement that Andrews had a "sore shoulder" that would prohibit him from further World Series play.

Andrews also had to sign at the bottom of the statement, saying that he agreed with the diagnosis. Later Andrews admitted that Finley had threatened to "destroy me in baseball" unless he signed.

Commissioner Bowie Kuhn rejected the request to put Andrews on the disabled list, saying that Andrews had suffered no injury. Andrews was reinstated.

A's manager Dick Williams was infuriated by the shenanigans, and resigned at the end of the series, moments after winning it.

Andrews came back to play the fourth game, in New York. After grounding out as a pinch hitter, he received a thunderous ovation from the Shea Stadium crowd. Andrews retired at the end of the series.

• • •

Who was the only pitcher to play for both the Seattle Pilots and the Seattle Mariners?
Diego Segui.

Segui pitched for the Pilots in their only year of existence (1969), compiling a 12-6 record, with a 3.35 ERA — second best on the staff. Then after bouncing around the majors, including a tour with the A's in which he led the

AL with a 2.56 ERA, he wound up with the Mariners again in their first year, 1977. Segui lost seven without a win, posting a 5.68 ERA.

• • •

The Yankee-Dodger World Series matchup was an October tradition in the 1940s and 1950s. How many times did Brooklyn play the Yankees in the fall classic before finally winning a World Series?
1955 was a year no Brooklyn Dodger fan will ever forget. After five unsuccessful tries at beating the hated Yankees, the Bums beat them in an exciting seven-game series.

It looked as though the Yankees would win the sixth meeting between the two teams. The Yankees were victorious in the first two games of the series, winning 6-5 and 4-2. The Dodgers came back to win the next three games, scoring 21 runs off Yankee pitching.

Dodger bats were cooled by Whitey Ford in the sixth game as the Yankees knocked Karl Spooner out of the box in the first inning and went on to win, 5-1.

That set up the seventh game of the Series. In the sixth inning with Johnny Podres nursing a 2-0 lead, Sandy Amoros made a spectacular catch in left field to rob Yogi Berra of an extra-base hit. He then fired to second to erase Gil McDougald for the double play. Podres settled down after that, shutting out the Yankees and giving Brooklyn its only World Championship — and first Championship against the Yankees in six attempts.

The Yanks and Dodgers met five more times after that, and the Yanks won three of the five.

• • •

Flooding in Pittsburgh once created a strange ground rule. What was it?
On July 4, 1902, water was knee-deep in Pittsburgh's Exposition Park.

But the scheduled game was played anyway — with a caveat.

Anyone who hit a ball into the water (named Lake Dreyfuss after the Pirates' owner) would be awarded an automatic double.

• • •

Babe Ruth is not remembered for his defensive skills, but they were excellent, nonetheless. Can you recall his best fake?

Once in Detroit, Ruth was playing left field, when the Tiger batter hit a long fly ball straight to him. Ruth knew he could catch it, but he wanted to also nail Charlie Gehringer, standing on second. Ruth pretended the fly had somehow cleared the wall, looking dejected. Gehringer, seeing Ruth's dejection, took off for home. Ruth then woke up, neatly caught the ball, and trapped Gehringer off second for the inning-ending double play.

• • •

At the age of 34 a Canadian member of the New York Yankees was deferred from military duty, yet his sense of patriotism burned so deeply that he joined the Navy in 1943. Name that outfielder.

George Selkirk of Huntsville, Ontario was one of the more nimble players of the late 1930s and was suitably nicknamed "Twinkletoes." He was a star for the Yankees and before enlisting played for their 1942 championship team. Others on that squad included Bill Dickey, Aaron Robinson, Ken Sears and Ken Silvestri, all catchers who joined the armed forces, not to mention the immortal Joe DiMaggio. Selkirk, who played in no less than six World Series, never returned to the big leagues.

• • •

2

1. Name the only two players to win the triple crown twice.
2. The first AL Triple Crown winner was in the league's first year. He was a second baseman. Who was he?
3. In 1947, the Rookie of the Year award was presented for the first time. Who won it?
4. How many records did Reggie Jackson set in 1977?
5. Which major league team was first to win 100 games in one season?
6. What is the least number of wins with which a team has won the pennant?
7. What is the least number of wins a team has needed to win the pennant since 1900?
8. Which team's wins were furthest from the second-place team?
9. What is the record for the most strikeouts in one game?
10. Rennie Stennett once had seven hits in a nine-inning game, but that's not the record for most hits in a game. What is?

Answers begin on page 172.

Zealandia, Saskatchewan's contribution to the Major Leagues was Aldon Jay (Lefty) Wilkie. For which team did he play?

For three seasons — 1941, 1942 and 1946 — Lefty Wilkie pitched for the Pittsburgh Pirates. He left the club after the 1942 campaign to join the armed forces and returned to toil for one more year in the bigs. In that span he totalled eight wins, eleven losses and a 4.59 earned run average. Nobody else in the history of Zealandia can make that statement.

• • •

Name the player who retreated from second to first base, thereby causing the baseball establishment to rewrite the rules.

Germany Schaefer was called "The Clown Prince of Baseball" for good reason. The Washington Senators infielder was given to bursts of bizarre behavior that confounded teammates and foe alike.

Once in a game against the Chicago White Sox, Schaefer reached first on a single and then stole second. A teammate, Clyde Milan, was already on third. To the astonishment of everyone in the ball park Germany waited for the next pitch and then raced *back to first*. While the astonished Chicago pitcher wound up for the next pitch Schaefer sped to second once again for another perfect steal but, this time, the White Sox decided to do something about it. The catcher fired the ball to the first baseman who touched the base, hoping to inspire the umpire to flash the "out" sign — but nothing happened. The first baseman then threw to the second baseman who touched the bag, then touched the grinning Schaefer but still the umpire did not call an "out." When the White Sox protested the umpire pointed out that Schaefer was where he rightfully belonged and that he was safe indeed. The umpire's logic went this way: when Schaefer stole second the first time it made him a legal occupant of the bag, and that if he had been touched with the ball while he was running from second to first then he would have been out. But since nobody had touched him he was quite safe on second.

Meanwhile, the official scorer ruled that although Germany had stolen three bases he was legally entitled to only one. And to prevent any future "triple steals" the rulemakers wrote an amendment stipulating that whereas a player may advance at will, he cannot retreat a base.

Of course, Germany always could say that he had forced a change in the rule book; and he did. "Getting one bird to pull a boner, that's something," he confessed. "But when you get nine guys out there on the field teaming up on a boner — say, that's something."

And it was.

• • •

Jeff Tesreau, an accomplished spitball pitcher with the New York Giants, once got his comeuppance from the Philadelphia Phillies. How did they foil him?
Otto Knabe and Mike Doolan of the Phillies huddled one day in an effort to dope out a way to stop the vaunted Tesreau. In those days baseballs were kept in play until they were so battered they were replaced. Thus, a ball could remain in action as long as five innings before a replacement was summoned.

At the end of the first inning, after the Phillies had retired, few noticed that the ball was tossed to Knabe. This happened again after the second and third inning as well. By the end of the third inning an unusual development occurred; the usually redoubtable Tesreau asked to be relieved and one look at him told the reason why: his lips were swollen to such an extent that the upper was just under his nostrils, interfering with his breathing. His teammates wondered what had happened but Knabe knew the answer. He had doctored the ball with capsicum salve.

Every time Tesreau kissed it, he was kissing his game away.

• • •

In their World Championship year of 1969, the New York Mets swept the Pirates in an important September doubleheader, 1-0 and 1-0. What was unusual about this sweep?

The Mets' only two runs of the day were driven in by the starting pitchers.

In the opener, Jerry Koosman, who hit a mere .048 that year, drove in the Mets' only run with a base hit in the fifth inning. Koosman went the distance in the three-hit shutout.

The offense in the nightcap came from the bat of Don Cardwell, who hit 15 homers over his 14-year pitching career. Cardwell gave up four hits, but was lifted in the eighth. He drove in the winning run in the second.

• • •

In the Washington Senators' final game, which Senator pitcher received credit for the decision?

Nobody. The Senators forfeited the game to Yankees, 9-0.

Actually the Senators were one out away from winning the game. Down 5-1 after five innings, the Senators came back, scoring six unanswered runs to lead, 7-5.

With one out remaining in the contest and Joe Grzenda pitching, many of the 14,460 fans stormed the field and disrupted play. They didn't want to see the Senators win their final game ever! After ten minutes, the fans got their wish; the umpires forfeited the game to the Yankees. Since pitchers cannot get a decision on a forfeited game, no Senator pitcher won or lost the game. But then, no Yankee pitcher won it.

• • •

Who was the only big-league player ever to be expelled from a game for eating popcorn?

It was common practice for Germany Schaefer, who played and clowned for five AL teams from 1901 to 1918, to sit in the coaching box with a bag of popcorn whenever he wanted to express his dislike for the opposing team. He would sit in the box with his popcorn and stare blankly at the sky, implying that he found the whole game terribly boring. It was Schaefer's public sign of his displeasure.

One day in 1912, Schaefer was playing against Chicago when he appeared in the coaching box with a huge bag of popcorn. Umpire Silk O'Loughlin found the act very offensive and ordered Schaefer off the field, claiming that Schaefer detracted from the seriousness of the game.

Schaefer remains the only major-league player ever to be thrown out of a game for chewing popcorn.

* * *

On three occasions two pitchers have combined for a no-hitter. Name the three sets of pitchers, and the teams for which they pitched.

Babe Ruth and Ernie Shore of the Red Sox, Steve Barber and Stu Miller of the Orioles, and John "Blue Moon" Odom and Francisco Barrios of the White Sox all combined efforts and skill for no-hitters.

Odom and Barrios combined to blank the Oakland A's, 2-0, on July 28, 1976. Odom pitched the first five innings, but issued nine walks. Since the A's thrived on walks and baserunning, Odom needed help. Barrios, who died in a recent car accident, came in to pitch the final four innings, issuing two more walks. The Sox were aided by three double plays. Curiously, the victor was Odom, who had been a star for the A's in the World Championship seasons.

Barber and Miller weren't as lucky when they teamed up for their no-hitter on April 30th, 1967, against the Tigers in Detroit. Barber was clinging to a 1-0 lead when he became unglued. With a man on third, Barber threw a wild pitch, giving up the tying run. Later in the inning, the Orioles made an error that cost them another run. Stu Miller came in to get the final out, but the Orioles lost the no-hitter, 2-1.

The oddest one of all took place on June 23, 1917. The great Babe Ruth walked the first Senator batter of the game in Washington, and then got involved in a heated argument with the plate umpire. The umpire heard enough, and tossed out Ruth. Ernie Shore, sitting in the dugout, was told go out and pitch until a reliever could get warmed up. He threw out the runner, and then retired the next 26 men he faced for the most unusual perfect game on record. Shore was credited with a perfect game . . . that he didn't start.

On September 28, 1975, four pitchers, Vida Blue, Glenn Abbott, Paul Lindblad and Rollie Fingers of the A's, teamed up to no-hit the Angels, 4-0.

• • •

How did a home run by Buck Freeman of the Washington Senators send a man to jail?

One day Freeman hit a home run over the fence during a game with the Philadelphia Athletics. After the ball cleared the fence it landed square on the head of an innocent passer-by who was knocked unconscious before he knew what had hit him.

A concerned policeman saw what had happened and rushed to the victim in an attempt to revive him. As the man regained consciousness he looked at the club-carrying policemen, put two and two together (or so he thought), and swung a fist at the astonished cop. The gentleman had assumed, of course, that the policeman was responsible for the lump on his head.

Before the gendarme could explain, the irate citizen shouted: "You tried to murder me. You cracked me on the head and I hadn't done a thing." He kicked the cop in the shin and was biting his forearm when another policeman arrived. The two of them finally subdued the poor baseball-struck pedestrian and finally, with the aid of a third cop, took him to jail. After he had promised to maintain decorum, the victim was told what had really happened and released from jail.

• • •

When was a night watchman awarded a special day at Cleveland's municipal stadium?

In 1948 night watchman Joe Early wrote a letter to the *Cleveland Press* asking why it was that teams gave "days" to overpaid stars — who didn't really need money, record players and cars — instead of to loyal fans like himself, who were in need. He signed the letter "Good Old Joe Early."

Bill Veeck, then running the Indians, saw Early's logic. He called the *Press* to obtain Early's address, then told the night watchman to be at the ball park on a certain night. Veeck was also able to keep the press from leaking his plan.

On the appointed night, Veeck opened the show by giving away 20,000 fresh Hawaiian orchids to the first 20,000 women who came through the turnstiles. Then "Good Old Joe Early" was honored. First he was given "a house in Early American architecture" — whereupon an outhouse was wheeled onto the field. Next they announced the presentation of "an Early automobile." A Model-T from a circus, complete with explosions, collapsing fenders and backfires, limped onto the field. Livestock followed the car.

After the fun was over, the *real* gifts came. A new Ford convertible, and a truck filled with refrigerator, washing machine, luggage, wristwatches and clothes — all from local merchants — were part of the largesse. Early became a local celebrity for a time, appearing on TV and radio.

• • •

Can you name the major leaguer who set a record by fanning in his first 14 plate appearances?

Billy Sunday of the Chicago White Stockings made his major league debut on May 22, 1883. He struck out in his first 14 appearances, but hung on until 1890, coming up with a .248 lifetime average. In 1890, he gave up baseball to become an evangelist, and gained great fame from his strident, well-publicized, fundamentalist sermons.

● ● ●

This player was a pitching failure but an offensive smash, becoming the first man to hit over .400 three times. Who was he?

Five years after his pitching career ended in a miserable 3-11 mark, Jesse Burkette of the Cleveland Spiders hit .423 in 1895, and .410 the year after. Combined with a .402 mark in 1899, he hit .341 overall in his 16-year career, and was elected to the Hall of Fame in 1946.

● ● ●

When did six teammates try to carry a player to first base?

In 1917, when the Brooklyn Dodgers were earning their nickname as the "DAFFINESS BOYS," they were playing a game against the Giants. Jack Coombs, the Dodger pitcher, was on second and Hi Myers on first. Brooklyn shortstop Ollie O'Mara, he of the short temper, was at the plate.

O'Mara was ordered to bunt and proceeded to oblige by dropping one in front of Giants' catcher Red Dooin, who leaped on the ball and pegged it to third in an effort to head off Coombs. The toss was wild and rolled to the fence, where outfielder George Burns retrieved it.

But O'Mara never ran to first. He looked over his shoulder, saw Dooin pick up the ball and shrieked "Foul!" at umpire Hank O'Day. When the umpire replied that it was a fair ball, O'Mara continued the argument, several decibels higher, while his teammates rounded the bases.

Meanwhile, a half-dozen Dodgers raced from the dugout, grabbed O'Mara and tried to carry him to first but the enraged shortstop lunged back at the umpire, ignoring his teammates. Another squad of Dodgers came out and tried to convoy O'Mara to first but they, too, failed. Finally, the group of them got him away from the umpire and headed toward first, but it was all too late. The Giants had relayed the ball from left field and O'Mara was tagged out ten feet from the bag.

• • •

In 1910, two players were involved in the closest batting title race ever, resulting in the expulsion of a major league manager and player-coach from baseball. Who were the players and what were the circumstances?

Ty Cobb of the Tigers and Napoleon Lajoie of the Indians fought a tough but friendly race for the batting title in the 1910 season. On the final day of the chase, Lajoie went 8-for-9 in a double-header against the St. Louis Browns; half of his hits came on bunts. He and Cobb finished the season with .384 averages. Cobb refused to share the crown, and accused St. Louis Browns' manager Jack O'Connor and player-coach Harry Howell of conspiring against him in favor of Lajoie, who was a less fiery individual than Cobb. Cobb pointed out that Lajoie had four bunt base hits.

AL President Ban Johnson banned O'Connor and Howell from baseball, declaring Cobb the official winner with a .3848 average while Lajoie finished second with a .3841 mark.

In 1981, the *Sporting News* started research on the incident to while away the baseball strike. They determined that the American League had erred in computing box scores, and taken hits away from Lajoie, and given extra ones to Cobb. This was due to the slipshod manner of keeping records by hand. The *News* determined that Lajoie was the rightful winner of the 1910 batting crown by two points, and that Cobb's streak of 9 straight batting titles had to be snapped. The Baseball Commissioner's office ignored the *Sporting News'* findings.

• • •

Which World Series between the Giants and Yankees was ended with a fielding classic?

The 1921 World Series was unusual in that it was one of the few decided on a best-five-out-of-nine basis. In this tournament the Giants were leading four games to three. In the eighth game they carried a 1-0 lead into the ninth inning.

All the Giants needed at this point was to produce three outs — while holding the Yankees scoreless — and they would have the championship. Pitching for the Giants, Art Nehf retired Babe Ruth on a groundout, but he walked the next batter, Aaron Ward.

With a runner on first and one out, Nehf faced Frank Baker who promptly smashed a grounder between second baseman Johnny Rawlings and first baseman George Kelly. Realizing that he had no chance to field the ball, Rawlings hurled himself at it. The amazing dive enabled Rawlings to get in front of the ball, which carommed off his chest. He picked it up and while still horizontal tossed to Kelly who grabbed the ball before Baker reached first.

Watching the play, the speeding Ward thought he had a chance to highball it to third base. But the moment he made the put out at first, Kelly took the long-shot chance of nailing Ward enroute to third. The first baseman pegged the ball 127 feet, from first to third, where Frankie Frisch, the Giants third baseman, was awaiting the throw — and Ward.

About ten feet from the bag, Ward decided to insure his safety by entering with a blistering slide as the ball entered Frisch's mitt. Ward slammed into Frisch and third base almost simultaneously, causing a dust storm that almost obliterated the third base umpire, who watched Frisch tumble over and over through the dust.

Frisch finally regained his equilibrium and, to the utter disbelief of all, had kept the ball clawed in his hand. The umpire delivered a resounding "OUT!" suitable to the occasion and the Giants had won themselves a World Series.

• • •

How did a haircut cost Stengel a $200 fine?

In 1921 Casey was traded from the Philadelphia Phillies to the New York Giants. Prior to his first game with the new team, Stengel thought it would be appropriate to have his hair cut. "Give it the works!" Casey implored the barber. When the tonsorial artist finished his job he gilded Stengel's locks with an overdose of high-smelling hair tonic, which suited the new Giant just fine.

That day Stengel came to bat and was immediately sent to the dirt with a spate of brush-back pitches. Casey was furious and, finally, dashed to the mound where he and the pitcher slugged away. When they were separated, Stengel was banished from the game.

The forlorn Casey trudged to the dugout and was heading for the clubhouse when he encountered his manager, John McGraw. The boss' nose wrinkled and he got a whiff of Stengel's hair pomade. "You're fined $200," McGraw intoned.

"All that for just getting into a fight?" asked Stengel.

"Dammit, no," McGraw replied. "I'm fining you $200 for reporting for play smelling of cheap gin!"

• • •

A teammate's mental error cost Lou Gehrig the home run title in 1931. Who was the culprit?

Lyn Lary of the New York Yankees was on first base in Washington when Gehrig stepped to the plate against the

Senators. Lou and Babe Ruth were tied in the home run derby with 46 apiece as the season reached the finish line. Gehrig hit a line drive that landed in the left-center field bleachers but rebounded back to the playing field.

Outfielder Harry Rice picked it up and lobbed it toward the infield. Lary, who was running on the hit, did not see anything of the ball until Rice made the throw. He mistakenly believed that Rice had caught the ball for the third out and stopped running for the plate. Instead, he jogged over to the dugout for a drink of water before taking his position on the field.

Ignoring Lary, Gehrig rounded the bases and sped across home plate. He thought he had himself a home run but, in fact, he was ruled out by the umpires for having passed a runner. Lary, unfortunately, never did reach home plate.

• • •

Who was the catcher who mistakenly decided to try to catch a baseball dropped from a passing blimp?
The intrepid player in question was Joe Sprinz who, in 1939, was playing minor-league ball in San Francisco. Sprinz said he could catch a ball dropped from a greater height than any other ball player. On August 3, 1939 he arranged with a blimp crew operating over Treasure Island, California, to drop the baseball.

Sprinz was waiting underneath when the ball left the gondola of the blimp and plummeted at a speed estimated at more than 140 miles per hour. When the ball struck Sprinz' glove it hit so hard that it bounced the glove into the catcher's face, cracked an eight-tooth plate in his mouth and lacerated his lips, nose and cheek. X-rays at the hospital later revealed that he had also fractured his upper jaw.

It was the last time Joe Sprinz attempted to field a ball dropped from a blimp.

• • •

3

FAMOUS SECONDS

1. Ty Cobb holds the highest lifetime batting average, at .367. Who's second and what's his average?
2. Stan Musial holds the record for most extra-base hits with 1377 in a career. Who's second and how many does he have?
3. Mantle and Maris have the highest single season home run 1-2 punch, with 115 between them (54 and 61 respectively). What tandem is second?
4. Hack Wilson holds the single season record for RBI's with 190. Who's second and how many does he have?
5. Babe Ruth has the highest lifetime HR-per-at-bat ratio among players with 300 or more HR's. Who's second?
6. Another of Ruth's records is reaching first base safely the most times in one season — 379. Who's second and how many times did he reach first safely? (Coincidentally, this same person holds the record for giving up the most runs in one game with 13.)
7. Wes Ferrell holds the career record for home runs by a pitcher with 37. Who's second and how many did he hit?
8. Why does Joe DiMaggio's 56-game hitting streak count as a famous second?
9. Why does Babe Ruth's famous "Called Shot" count as a famous second?

Answers begin on page 172.

How did a pair of glasses cost Dan MacFayden of the Pittsburgh Pirates a $100 fine?

Pitching for Pittsburgh in 1940 against the Philadelphia Phillies, MacFayden had two strikes on batter Bobby Bragan with two men out in the ninth inning. MacFayden blazed the next pitch down the middle and figured he had struck out the batter. But umpire Bill Klem called it a ball.

The irate MacFayden cussed and moaned until Klem finally headed for the mound to calm the unnerved pitcher. Sadly, MacFayden misinterpreted the umpire's intentions and sneered as Klem reached the pitcher's side.

Without further ado, MacFayden removed his glasses and handed them to Klem. "Take 'em," he said. "You need 'em more than I do."

Klem ordered MacFayden to the showers and the following day the pitcher learned that he had been fined $100 for his offering.

• • •

In a game at Montreal two baseballs were in play simultaneously. How did that happen?

The Rochester Red Wings were playing the Montreal Royals during an International League game at Montreal in 1940 with umpire Al Barlick behind the plate.

Montreal led 5-2 but Rochester rallied and had the bases loaded when the next batter lined the ball to centerfield. After the first two runners crossed the plate the third runner attempted to do likewise. The play at home was close but umpire Barlick ruled the runner out. Meanwhile, Montreal pitcher Bill Crouch, who had backed up the play, noticed a ball on the ground, picked it up and tossed it to third, attempting to get the Rochester batter, who was hoping to stretch a double into a triple. The throw was late but the Rochester manager rushed out of the dugout and charged that his runner at the plate was safe. "The catcher dropped the ball," he insisted, "so the runner's safe."

But Barlick shook his head, and the catcher put in his two cents and showed the ball still warm in his hand from the putout.

"Wait a minute," yelled the Rochester manager, pointing to the Montreal third baseman. "He's got a ball." Then, grabbing the catcher by the arm, "and *he's* got a ball. What's goin' on here?"

The umpire then explained. "I'll tell you what's going on. When I signalled that runner out, the jerk of my arm snapped a ball out of my pocket. That's the one Crouch threw to third. The guy is out at home, just as I said."

Although he had settled the argument for the moment, Barlick, then a young aspiring umpire, had expected that there would be negative reverberations from the league office. Sure enough, two days later he received a telegram; and it was from the league office. The news, however, was not bad. He had been promoted from the minors to the National League. At 25, Barlick had become the youngest umpire in National League history!

• • •

How did a foul ball hit by a Boston Red Sox batter become a 40-foot triple?

Jake Jones of the Red Sox took a swipe at a pitch thrown by Fred Sanford of the St. Louis Browns during the 1947 season. The ball rolled slowly toward third base as Sanford raced to field the sphere. When Sanford realized he couldn't make the play he disgustedly tossed his glove at the ball. Sanford did not realize that the ball had slipped over the foul line and would have been a strike. But the ball was struck by the glove and Umpire Cal Hubbard awarded Jones a triple.

It was a legitimate call since the rule states that in the event a ball is hit by a deliberately thrown glove, whether it's in foul territory or not, the batter receives three bases.

• • •

When did Lenny Randle get blacked out and find he wasn't alone in the dark?

At precisely 9:34 pm, on July 13, 1977, Lenny Randle of the New York Mets stood at the plate in Shea Stadium, facing Ray Burris of the Chicago Cubs.

As Burris went into his windup, in the bottom of the sixth, all the lights in the stadium flashed off as if a massive switch had been thrown.

Randle said, "I thought, 'God, I'm gone,' I thought for sure He was calling me. I thought it was my last at-bat."

Moments later, emergency power came on for the corridors, ramps, and organ in the stadium, but the rest of New York City had been blacked out by power lines breaking . . . and would remain so for 25 hours.

The Mets alertly closed the concession stands to prevent people from getting tanked on beer, and then had the players drive their cars onto the field.

Once this was done, the Mets went through infield drills . . . without a ball. After the "drill," the organist started a sing-along, and the 22,000 fans responded by belting out "White Christmas" in the 90° heat. The players congregated along the railings to talk with fans and sign autographs. Fans with cars started offering lifts to those without.

The Cubs, meanwhile, boarded their bus to drive back in the dark to the Waldorf-Astoria Hotel. There, the management issued the players candles so they could make the 17-floor climb to their rooms.

It was not the first time an electrical failure had halted a game, of course. George Kell recalled an incident in Washington. Kell had a 2-2 count "and the pitcher was in his windup when all the lights suddenly went out. I quickly hit the dirt. I must have stayed down there a good minute when I began to feel foolish and started to get up. Just as I did, the lights came on again. It was quite a sight. Every outfielder and infielder, even the catcher, was flat on the ground. The only guy standing was the pitcher. He knew where the ball was."

• • •

When did the Detroit Tigers stage a sympathy strike for Ty Cobb?

Even though Ty Cobb was a fairly detested character throughout baseball, his teammates respected him for his hard hitting and hustling play. When Cobb was suspended in 1912 for attacking a New York heckler, the Tigers warned the American League that they would go on strike until Cobb was reinstated.

On May 18, 1912, the Tigers, complete with Cobb, took the field in Philadelphia to play Connie Mack's A's.

The umpires ordered Cobb off the field. The Tigers, including such stars as Sam Crawford, George Moriarty, Davy Jones, Jim Delahanty, George Mullin and Bill Burns, followed Cobb off the field.

The Tigers faced a forfeit and a $5,000 fine for the owner. Manager Hughey Jennings pleaded for time. Connie Mack, ever-gracious, gave Jennings time to assemble a scratch crew to face the defending world champion A's.

That afternoon, the Tigers' hotel was besieged by semi-pro players answering Jennings' call for help. $50 for the game was more than a semi-pro player made in a year back then, and at least 700 players showed up. Jennings picked out 25 players, and had his two ancient coaches play as well.

With this crew, he set off to the ball park. The two coaches played first base and behind the plate, while Al Travers, a future priest, pitched. William Charles Leinhauser was reduced in the boxscore to "L'n'h's'r" but he did play center field. Manager Jennings pinch hit for exercise.

The A's took the game seriously, and behind Jack Coombs and Herb Pennock, they won handily, 24-2. The "Tigers" made 10 errors, gave up 25 hits, and only the two old coaches — setting a record for the oldest men to play in a major league game — scored for the Tigers, mostly because the A's let them go around the bases for old time's sake!

AL President Ben Johnson got the point. He reduced Cobb's suspension and fine — but each Tiger was fined $100, twice Cobb's fine. They were ordered to play or face expulsion.

The Tigers went back to work, but at least William Charles Leinhauser, Al Travers, Billy Maharg, and a score of other unknowns were able to truthfully say they had once played for the Detroit Tigers.

• • •

Dodger fans once showed their support for manager Leo Durocher in an unusual way. What was it?
When Durocher was fined $25 for arguing with umpire Tom Dunn, the Brooklyn fans considered it such an injustice that they collected 2500 pennies to pay off the fine.

Another unusual fine occurred when outfielder Goose Goslin took his argument with umpire Bill Klem into an elevator in a Detroit hotel, and was hit with a $50 foul-language fine.

Cleveland Indian pitcher Johnny Allen persisted in wearing a tattered sweatshirt, which made it difficult for batters to see the ball. The league ordered him to change shirts. When Allen didn't, he was slapped with a $200 fine.

Once, Texas Ranger third baseman Lenny Randle hit his manager, Frank Lucchessi, in spring training, before the viewing fans in Florida.

Randle was upset about not being able to win a regular job. The Pompano Beach fans, who saw the battle, were equally upset.

Randle found himself with a record $10,000 fine, and was shipped to the New York Mets, where he had his finest season ever, hitting .304 and stealing 33 bases.

Recently, Dodger pitcher Steve Howe was fined $53,000,

a month's pay, for drug abuse. The money went to drug rehabilitation charities.

• • •

Lyman Bostock suffered a horrifying death in 1978. How did it happen?

While visiting relatives in Gary, Indiana, Bostock was sitting in a car with a female relative. Suddenly the lady's estranged boyfriend appeared with a gun, and he dispatched Bostock — the wrong target — with several bullets. The boyfriend had been aiming at the woman.

Bostock died the same day, September 23, 1978. In April that year, he had offered to return his entire salary to the California Angels, because he believed he had not performed up to his abilities. The Angels rejected the offer, so Bostock had turned the money over to charity.

• • •

Why did outfielder Frank Thomas quit reading *The Power of Positive Thinking* when he was with the New York Mets in 1962?

Thomas had played for last-place teams in 11 of his first 15 seasons in the majors and decided that *The Power of Positive Thinking* might help both him and the lowly Mets. But one day he suddenly stopped reading the book. His roommate found that puzzling and asked Thomas about it. The outfielder shot back: "I was crazy about the book. I was sure it would help my hitting, until a thought occurred to me: What if the pitchers had read it, too? That's when I quit on it."

• • •

How did Cardinal Catcher Joe Garagiola wind up in the Pittsburgh Pirates dugout while running out a bunt?

Tough Rip Sewell was pitching for the Pirates when Garagiola was with the St. Louis Cardinals. Garagiola objected to a Sewell brush-back pitch and bunted the next one down the first-base line. Joe had hoped to bowl over Sewell but the pitcher was one step ahead of him. When Garagiola lumbered down upon him, Sewell threw a heavy block at Joe and sent him reeling right into the Pirates' dugout.

"Next thing I knew," said Garagiola, "one Pirate had me by one leg, another by the other leg, and somebody was saying, 'Make a wish.'"

• • •

Why did pitcher Warren Spahn insist upon hanging his plaque as top hurler of 1961 in manager Birdie Tebbets' office?
As Spahn explained to his manager: "The next time I have a bad day I want you to be reminded I can't be as lousy as I looked!"

• • •

Who hit the most career homers against the Expos?
The man who took Expo pitchers downtown most often was Pittsburgh's Willie Stargell, who victimized them 37 times.

He hit 22 shots in Montreal, and 15 in Pittsburgh. On May 20, 1978, Stargell unloaded a 535-foot homer off Wayne Twitchell, which landed on a chair in the second deck over right field. The seat was replaced by a gold one to commemorate the blast, the longest in Olympic Stadium.

Coincidentally, the shot was Stargell's 407th, tying him with Duke Snider on the all-time list. Duke Snider was broadcasting the game for the Expos.

• • •

Who was the first ballplayer to wear glasses on the field?
William Henry White of the early National League won 227 games for three teams from 1877 to 1886, while wear-

ing glasses. But the first major-leaguer of the modern era to wear specs on the ballfield was pitcher Lee "Specs" Meadows, of the St. Louis Cardinals. The Cards continued to be a home for players with glasses, as Meadows was followed by George "Specs" Toporcer, an infielder who lasted eight years, hitting .279.

St. Louis maintained the tradition with batting champion Chick Hafey, who led the National League in batting in 1931. He was forced to wear glasses due to sinus trouble.

The St. Louis Browns had the first catcher to wear glasses. Clint Courtney, who lasted eleven years in the major leagues as a clutch hitter and a strong handler of pitchers.

Since the umpire's reputation rests almost solely on eyesight, glasses worn would be a certain invitation to criticism.

In 1972, '73 and '74, bespectacled players were awarded the American League's Most Valuable Player award. They were Richie Allen, Reggie Jackson and Jeff Burroughs respectively. All attributed their success to wearing glasses.

• • •

Who was the first American leaguer to steal over 100 bases?

Not Ty Cobb, whose best mark was 97.

Rickey Henderson, in 1980, his second year in the Majors, stole 100 bases, becoming the first American leaguer in its history to do so. He followed the triumph in 1981, the year of the strike, by leading the American league again in stolen bases, with 56. In 1982, he led the American League for the third straight year, by stealing a record 130 bases, breaking the single-season mark set by Lou Brock, in 1974, with 118.

Asked by a reporter how to stop Henderson's thievery,

Detroit Tiger pitching coach Roger Craig said, "He can't steal first base, can he?"

• • •

What was the highest uniform number worn by a player in the regular season?
In 1977, Willie Crawford, a journeyman outfielder, asked for and was granted Number 99 from the Oakland A's. He thus passed New York Giant Bill Voiselle, who came from Ninety-Six, South Carolina, and had that pasted on his uniform, in 1944.

In 1981, Billy Martin had over 100 players at the Oakland A's spring training, but none of the players in the eighties or higher made the club. They were in camp so that Martin could look at them before they went to their minor league teams.

The lowest recorded numbers were Paul Dade's Double Zero, 00, with the Cleveland Indians, Bobby Bonds' Double Zero with the St. Louis Cardinals, and George Scott's Double Zero with the Kansas City Royals.

When Al Oliver went to the Texas Rangers, he requested and was given Number 0. He was seeking a new start, and fan recognition for his considerable batting talents. Besides, his last name started with a capital O, O for Oliver.

• • •

A pinch-runner once hit a Grand Slam! How did this happen?
In 1958, Gene Stephens was sent in to pinch run for Ted Williams. Stephens was immediately cut down in a force play, but the Red Sox were hot and the rally continued until Stephens came up to bat. Manager Billy Jurges let him hit, and Stephens responded with a grand slam. Boston won the game, 13-3.

• • •

Hank Greenberg received some illegal help from coach Del Baker in hitting home runs. Do you recall what it was?

Del Baker called nearly every pitch for Greenberg in the '30s and '40s. The code was in the first word Baker yelled. Baker would call, "Come on Hank, hit it," and Greenberg would wait for a fastball. If Baker used the word "get," Greenberg would set up for a curve. Baker was scrutinizing the opposing pitcher's signals to set up the call.

• • •

Master signal stealer Charlie Dressen was outstolen by Leo Durocher in 1951. Do you recall Durocher's system?

Leo Durocher's 13 1/2-game comeback with the Giants in 1951 was helped by a man who watched enemy players from a peephole in the centerfield clubhouse at the Polo Grounds. A buzzer in the dugout rang once for a fastball, and twice for a curve.

But when Bobby Thomson hit his famous "miracle shot" to win the pennant, he didn't know what was coming. Durocher insisted that if Thomson knew Ralph Branca's pitches, he would have swung at the first pitch — a fastball down the middle.

Dressen himself was a topnotch signal stealer. In the pre-game meeting before the 1953 All-Star game, Dressen was asked what signals were to be used by the National League squad. The Dodger manager bragged, "Don't worry about it men. I'll give each of you the signals used on your own team."

• • •

Who was the master of the hidden-ball trick?

Yankee shortstop Frankie Crosetti turned the hidden-ball trick into an art, with full cooperation from his pitcher, usually Lefty Gomez.

Crosetti would hide the ball in the back of his glove,

while keeping his palms visible to the runner to convince him that the pitcher had the ball. Meanwhile, Lefty Gomez, on the mound, would busily manicure the mound.

Crosetti would then talk to the nearest umpire to get the ump's attention. The runner, thinking the pitcher was ready, would take a lead of several steps, and then Crosetti would make the lunge — and the humiliating putout.

For humiliating it was — especially to Lou Boudreau, who told a radio interviewer one night that there was no excuse for anyone getting caught by the trick. The next day, Boudreau was nailed by White Sox third baseman Tony Cuccinello.

Indeed, Crosetti learned the play from Joe Cronin. Crosetti mastered it so well, he once caught Cronin.

But Bill Rogell, a Tiger infielder, was really chastised by the hidden-ball ploy. In the 1930s, Rogell delivered milk in the Chicago area. One of his stops was St. Louis Browns' infielder Oscar Melillo's home.

Rogell would arrive at Melillo's house at dawn, purposely rattle the bottles and yell, "Here's your milk, Melillo!"

Melillo had his revenge next season in a tie game. Rogell led off the tenth with a double. Once at second, Rogell took a lead, confident of scoring the go-ahead run. That was Melillo's cue.

Melillo walked over to Rogell, and said, "Remember how you used to wake me up in the morning by shouting, 'Here's your milk?'" Melillo asked. Rogell broke into a wide grin. "Well," Melillo concluded, "Here's the ball." And with a quick lunge, Rogell was tagged out.

● ● ●

Do you recall who hit the American League's first Grand Slam home run?
In 1916, Marty Kavanaugh of the Indians was sent in with the bases loaded. He hit a ball that flew past the Red Sox outfield, landed and rolled through the outfield fence. The

ball couldn't be recovered in time to make a play on anyone, and the Red Sox lost, 5-3.

* * *

Do you recall how teams started wearing gray uniforms on the road?
Connie Mack's Philadelphia A's played hard, aggressive baseball before the home fans in their white uniforms at the turn of the century, but on the road, they didn't want to spoil their clean whites.

Consequently, to elicit more effort, Mack had his men wear gray on the road, figuring they wouldn't mind dirtying the drab colours.

* * *

How did hilarious Brooklyn Dodger Babe Herman arrange to have an impersonator arrested by the police?
In the late 1920s the popular Dodgers outfielder got word that a character was making the rounds of New York night clubs and department stores pretending to be the Babe himself. Herman, who was notorious as one of the worst-fielding regulars in the majors, met with the police and offered a solution. "Next time anyone comes around claiming he's Babe Herman, take him outside and fungo a fly ball to him. If he catches it, have him arrested!"

* * *

Name the sports writer who later became commissioner of baseball.
Ford Frick. Even after he had moved into the commissioner's office Frick would often take pen in hand and dash off a few lines of poetry. But even in his days as a reporter Frick would be needled about his meanderings into the world of iambic pentameter. New York *Daily Mirror* sports editor Dan Parker once put Frick's rhymes into perspec-

tive when he wrote, "Ford Frick has never been mentioned for poet laureate — not even of Bulgaria!"

* * *

Which big league catcher explained baseball in terms of theology?

Wes Westrum of the New York Giants once explained that baseball "is like church." He amplified: "Many attend, but few understand."

* * *

How did an infielder allow four runs to score on a game-ending third out?

Once in the 1930s, with the bases loaded and two men out, a batter grounded to White Sox third baseman Zeke Bonura. Bonura picked up the ball, dropped it, picked it up again, and dropped it again. For a change of pace, he kicked the ball. When Bonura looked up, clutching the ball at last, all three runners had scored and the batter was heading towards third. Bonura fired to the pitcher covering third base — but the ball wound up in the dugout.

* * *

When did a runner try to score on a passed cast?

Houston's Norm Miller was standing on third when Atlanta Braves' catcher Bob Didier caught a low, outside fastball from sidearm reliever Cecil Upshaw. The ball knocked off a small, plastic cast Didier had been wearing on a sore finger, and the white device went spinning toward the backstop. Astros' third base coach Salty Parker mistook it for a ball, and sent Miller home.

Halfway there, Miller looked up to see Didier waiting for him with the ball. "Talk about a look of total disbelief!" said Braves' pitcher Gary Neibauer, watching on the sidelines. "Miller's eyes got as big as saucers and he just stood there as Didier tagged him out."

But one of the strangest fielding plays came in 1945.

Irvin Hall of the Philadelphia A's hit a line drive back to Senators' pitcher Dutch Leonard. Leonard caught the ball and then lost it. A hasty search revealed that the ball had lodged itself inside the pitcher's pants!

A's shortstop Eddie Joost played the comic role in 1948 when a grounder from Boston's Billy Goodman literally went up his sleeve, then dropped to his waist inside his uniform shirt. Ted Williams, the runner at third, was so overcome with laughter that he couldn't score.

* * *

When did a ballplayer hit an "inside-the-doghouse" home run?

The hapless Philadelphia A's were the victims when a Senator hit a long ball to center in Griffith Stadium. It rolled into a small doghouse-type box where the flag was stored. Socks Seibold poked his head and shoulders into the box in a vain search for the ball while the surprised Senator circled the bases for an inside-the-park home run.

* * *

In which major league ball park did a cow-milking contest take place before a game?

Baltimore's Municipal Stadium was the site of a contest in the early 1960s pitting Orioles pitcher Mike McCormick and infielder Bob Johnson. In time McCormick was declared the winner. Accepting his prize, the pitcher humbly told the ball park audience: "I could never have done it without the cow."

The Toronto Blue Jays won very few games in 1977, their inaugural season, but two members of the club won a cow-milking contest prior to a game in Minnesota.

Catcher Phil Roof and pitcher Chuck Hartenstein were the masters of the udders and seemed to be more at home with the bovines than they sometimes appeared on the diamond. Roof was the first player signed by Toronto.

* * *

QUICKIE QUIZ

4

MATCHING

Match these ballplayers of the 1970's with their real first names.

1. Rusty Staub	a. Claude
2. Tug McGraw	b. Johnnie
3. Dusty Baker	c. Daniel
4. Skip Lockwood	d. Albert
5. Sparky Lyle	e. Frank
6. Bud Harrelson	f. Jose
7. Coco Laboy	g. Derrel
8. Boots Day	h. Charles
9. Butch Hobson	i. Clell
10. Chris Chambliss	j. Carroll

Answers begin on page 172.

Who was the famed Irish tenor of the Brooklyn Dodgers?

First baseman Buddy Hassett played for the Dodgers in the late 1930s when Casey Stengel was managing the club. Hassett's voice was so highly regarded that he could sing professionally, but he also was a good ball player.

Once, when the Dodgers were training for their spring training base in Florida they encountered a mother and infant in the club car. The baby, apparently suffering from colic, cried incessantly from Newark to Baltimore.

Stengel finally got an idea; he suggested that Hassett's dulcet tones might lull the baby to sleep. "Madam," said Stengel, "I'm the manager of the Brooklyn Dodgers and this is my left-handed tenor singer, Buddy Hassett. He'll now sing your infant to sleep."

Without hesitation Hassett crooned a chorus of "Mighty Lak a Rose" and before he could reach the finale the baby was peacefully dozing in his mother's arms.

Stengel then returned to his seat and turned to one of the sportswriters who had been somewhat critical of him and observed: "I have my critics, but they can't say I don't get the most out of my players."

• • •

How did Hank Aaron turn a three-run homer into a one-run double?

In May, 1959, Harvey Haddix of the Pittsburgh Pirates pitched 12 perfect innings one night against the Milwaukee Braves, but the game was continuing on because the Pirates couldn't score either.

In the bottom of the 13th, the Braves' Felix Mantilla was safe on an error by Don Hoak. Eddie Matthews sacrificed Mantilla to second, and Henry Aaron was walked to set up an inning-ending double play. But Joe Adcock foiled the strategy by ripping the ball into the stands for a three-run, game-ending homer.

Mantilla scored, but Aaron, watching the ball go, was so

stunned, that he trotted directly to the Braves' dugout. Meanwhile, Adcock made the traditional home run trot. When he came home, he and Aaron were called out — Aaron for departing from the basepaths, Adcock for passing Aaron.

Adcock's three-run homer was turned into a one-run double. Furthermore, Haddix had lost his perfect game!

• • •

Can you recall which team had a .246 batting average, yet finished only two-and-a-half games out of first at the end of the season?

Bereft of Reggie Jackson, Catfish Hunter and Ken Holtzman, the 1976 Oakland A's chances were woefully slim.

To the surprise of the rest of the American League, however, the A's stole their way into second place in the AL West, setting a league record with 341 steals.

Most of the speed was generated by Don Baylor, Bill North and Bert Campaneris, all of whom stole over 50 bases, the first trio on a team to do so.

More speed was supplied by pinch-runner Herb Washington, a former world-class sprinter whom A's owner Charlie Finley hired to pinch-run and steal bases. He stole more than 20 bases without coming to bat! The A's fell six steals short of the Major League record set by the 1911 New York Giants, who pinched 347.

At the end of the year, the A's celebrated in their locker room, not because they'd won any titles, but rather because six of the stars — Joe Rudi, Sal Bando, Gene Tenace, Rollie Fingers, Bert Campaneris and Don Baylor — were all becoming free agents . . . and thus free from Charlie Finley's penurious contracts.

• • •

A native of Brandon, Manitoba is credited — or blamed,

as the case may be — for being the most successful exponent of "the emery ball." Who was that pitcher?

Russell Ford of the Buffalo Federals and the New York Highlanders (which eventually became the Yankees) perfected the emery ball. It was a freak pitch commonplace at the turn of the century, along with the shine ball and its distant cousin, the spitball. To produce an emery ball the pitcher roughened a portion of the ball's cover with a small piece of sandpaper, causing it to behave eratically in its flight to the batter. Ford, who enjoyed a six-year career in the majors, would keep the emery concealed in his glove.

For many seasons pitchers like Ford were able to escape detection, but the ruse was eventually discovered in 1914 when Jimmy Lavender of the Chicago Cubs made the mistake of fastening the sandpaper to his uniform. Baseball historian Harold Seymour noted that the age of the emery pitch ended then and there.

"Opposing pitchers soon wondered why Lavender seemed to be constantly scratching himself," wrote Seymour in *Baseball — The Golden Age*. An umpire finally investigated but Lavender fled.

"A ridiculous scene followed," Seymour added, "with the umpire refusing to give chase and Lavender refusing to come to him for inspection, knowing that under the rule then in effect he faced a five-dollar fine if he was caught with the goods. Suddenly, Hans Lobert of the Phillies, one of the fastest runners in the National League — so fast that he once raced a horse around the bases and lost by only a nose — dashed at Lavender and grabbed the evidence."

The emery pitch became a thing of the past — as did Russell Ford. A year later he was finished as a big-leaguer.

• • •

What was the importance of Al Gionfriddo's catch in the 1947 World Series?

Al Gionfriddo was never considered a prominent player,

but one play that he made off baseball's legendary Joe DiMaggio will always be remembered for the significant role it played in sixth game of the '47 classic.

The Yankees and the Dodgers were meeting in Yankee Stadium and the Dodgers desperately needed a miracle. They were behind 3 games to 2 and had to win to stay in the series.

At the bottom of the sixth, the Yanks came to bat trailing 8-5. Al Gionfriddo was playing in left field. George "Snuffy" Stirnweiss walked, followed by a single from Yogi Berra. Joe DiMaggio was next at the plate.

A home run would do it — would bring in three runs for the Yanks and tie the score 8-8. On the first pitch, Joe sent the ball sailing into left field. Since the ball was headed for the bullpen, it looked as if Joe had tied it up. But he wasn't counting on Al Gionfriddo. As the ball flew out across the field, Al outran it. Just in front of the bullpen fence, Al gave a diving leap for the ball and caught it, ending the inning. DiMaggio couldn't believe what he saw as he rounded second base. Disgusted, he headed for his position in center field.

The Dodgers were saved. Although the Yanks scored another run in the ninth, the game ended with the Yanks down, 8-6.

• • •

When baseball interest took hold in Canada during the 1870s one team emerged as the finest, not only in the dominion but all North America. Which city did it represent?

Guelph, Ontario. According to baseball historian Lee Allen, Canada was a center of baseball interest almost from the very invention of the pastime. Allen wrote in his book *The Hot Stove League*: "The Maple Leaves of Guelph, Ontario, constituted one of the finest professional nines of the 1870s."

• • •

Who was regarded as Canada's finest player in the 19th century?

James Edward (Tip) O'Neill, a native of Woodstock, Ontario, starred as an outfielder for the St. Louis Browns in the 1880s. His name made the record books in 1887 when his batting average soraed to .492. However, it should be noted that O'Neill was aided by a rule, in force only that year, that credited a base on balls as a hit. Nevertheless, even if the bases on balls were subtracted, O'Neill's batting figure would have been a handsome .442. O'Neill's average then is still four points higher than the next best mark of .438 reached by Hugh Duffy of the Boston Nationals in 1894.

• • •

A Canadian played a minor but significant role in the saga of super-hitter Ted Williams. Who was the pitcher and what was his role?

One of modern baseball's most notable accomplishments was Ted Williams' achievement of a .406 batting average for the Boston Red Sox in 1941. On September 28, 1941, the last day of the season, Williams average stood squarely at .400. His club was scheduled to play a double-header with the Philadelphia Athletics, which meant that "The Splendid Splinter" could finish below the coveted .400 mark. There was considerable speculation over the possibility of Williams deliberately being benched so that he would be assured of finishing with a .400 average.

Prior to the game Red Sox manager asked Williams if he wanted to sit it out. "I'll play," said Williams without hesitation. "I don't want anybody saying I got in through the back door."

The Red Sox' opponents were the lowly Philadelphia Athletics who had two Canadian pitchers, Dick Fowler and Phil Marchildon. It was the right-handed Fowler who faced Williams in the opening game of the double-header.

Fowler, who finished the season with a 1-2 record, could

not solve Williams that cold, damp afternoon in Philadelphia. On his first bat Williams singled sharply to right field. The second time The Splinter faced Fowler he pounded his 37th home run over the right field wall and out of the park. The ball carried 400 feet and was one of the longest shots Williams had ever hit. Athletics manager Connie Mack replaced Fowler with a lefthander, Porter Vaughan, before Williams came to bat again. It didn't matter. Williams smashed Vaughan's third pitch back through the box for his third straight hit. With Vaughan still pitching, Williams produced his fourth hit in a row, a line single over the first baseman's head. In all Williams had four hits in five times at bat in the first game.

Williams was urged to sit out the second game but he insisted upon playing again and this time went two-for-three, giving him a season-ending average of .406.

Fowler, incidentally, was removed in the fifth inning in a game that the Red Sox won, 12-11. Fowler was not credited with the loss. Philadelphia won the second game, 7-1.

• • •

Can you recall an umpire who called a perfect game without being aware of it?
On Father's Day 1964, before 32,026 fans, Jim Bunning of the Philadelphia Phillies sent down 27 Mets in a row to win the first perfect game in the National League's modern history.

Bunning also became the first pitcher to hurl a no hitter in each league. He was lucky enough to pitch his second no hitter in front of his wife and family at Shea Stadium. Umpire Ed Sudol had the tough job of calling balls and strikes that afternoon. When he was done, Met broadcaster Ralph Kiner interviewed Sudol, and congratulated him on arbiting the perfecto.

"I knew it was a no-hitter," Sudol said, "but I didn't

realize it was perfect. Do you mean I umpired a perfect game?"

Kiner, a Hall-of-Fame ballplayer, immediately quipped, "No, *you* didn't, but *it* was."

• • •

Do you recall when a fan attacked an umpire at Ebbets Field?

Passion for the Brooklyn Dodgers seemingly reached its peak on September 17, 1940. Umpire Billy Stewart ruled that Brooklyn Dodger second baseman Pete Coscarart had dropped the game-ending liner. Umpire-In-Chief George Magerkurth came from behind the plate to overrule Stewart, and thus, the Dodgers lost.

As angry fans swarmed the field, Magerkurth headed for his dressing room. Suddenly, a short powerfully built man leaped on Magerkurth, threw him to the ground and pummeled at the umpire's face.

When the case was brought before the magistrate, Magerkurth was out of Brooklyn on assignment and the charges were dropped.

Almost seven years later, on April 8th, 1947, pickpocket Frank Germano stood before Judge Samuel Leibowitz in Brooklyn on charges of picking pockets. As the Assistant District Attorney read out Germano's record, a litany of larceny, Leibowitz studied the defendant. He looked familiar.

"Haven't we met before?" asked Leibowitz.

"Maybe. I'm around a good deal," said Germano.

"You know," Leibowitz continued, "It seems to me that I've seen you in some crowd a few years ago — was it Ebbets Field?"

"Yes," the prisoner smiled. "I am a rabid Dodger rooter."

"Aren't you the fellow who knocked down umpire Magerkurth?"

The prisoner squared his shoulders and with pride in his voice announced, "Yes, Your Honor, I'm the man."

"You are a professional pickpocket," Leibowitz snapped. "Certainly if we're going to have our umpires assaulted at Ebbets Field, we don't want to have pickpockets doing it. I'm firmly convinced that it wasn't the umpire's decision that prompted you to knock him down. You undoubtedly had in mind to have a crowd collect and then have your partner go through their pockets. I'm going to send you to Sing Sing for a term of two-and-a-half to five years. On Sundays you can attend ball games up there at the Big House.

* * *

Which former Toronto Blue Jays hitting coach led the American League in slugging percentage in 1944?
Bobby Doerr, who played 14 seasons in the majors with the Boston Red Sox, captured the 1944 title with a slugging percentage of .528. But Doerr lost the batting championship by two points to Lou Boudreau of the Cleveland Indians.

* * *

Jeff Heath, an outfielder from Fort William, Ontario, played a pivotal role in one of baseball's greatest games, Bob Feller's first no-hitter. What was this Canadian's role?
On April 16, 1940 Bob (Rapid Robert) Feller of the Cleveland Indians faced the Chicago White Sox in the opening game of the American League season. Some 14,000 fans were in the stands at Comiskey Park when the 21-year-old Feller took the mound for the visitors.

The righthander already was being acclaimed as one of the finest young pitchers to come down the pike in years but on this afternoon he would permanently underline the point. Prior to the game Feller had complained of stiffness in his arm and as he warmed up there was little relief. He told his catcher, Rollie Hemsley, that he expected to get knocked out of the box.

The wind at Feller's back disturbed him, too. It is difficult to make a curve break in a tail wind, so Feller decided that he would have to accent his fast ball. And he did. In spades! One by one he mowed down the Chicago batters. With two out in the ninth, the White Sox still had not scored. Feller had struck out eight and walked five.

Taft Wright, a nemesis of Feller throughout the previous year, stepped to the plate and whacked a vicious ground ball between first baseman Hal Trosky and second baseman Ray Mack. Dashing to his left, Mack knocked down the ball with his gloved hand, dashed after it into short right field, retrieved the ball and fired to Trosky at first. Wright was out by a step!

The Indians won, 1-0, but the win wouldn't have been possible without Jeff Heath. In the fourth inning he singled and later scored on Hemsley's triple for the only run of the game.

• • •

The same Jeff Heath, later an outfielder for the Boston Braves, was involved in a bizarre incident involving the outfield wall at Wrigley Field in Chicago. Do you remember the episode?
On August 26,1948 the Braves were visiting the Chicago Cubs at Wrigley Field on Chicago's West Side. The Cubs' ball park has long been considered one of the most attractive in the majors, particularly because of the ivy that has climbed up the wall, giving it a rare arboreal look for a stadium.

When Phil Cavaretta of the Cubs come to bat on this day he stroked a line drive into the ivy as 24,000 fans cheered. Heath, who seemed to lose the trajectory of the ball momentarily, assumed that it had gotten stuck in the ivy.

Heath ran to the wall, looking for the ball in the ivy. "It was a strange sight," recalled author Ira L. Smith. "Heath stood in front of the wall and vigorously shook the ivy with both hands."

The outfielder was under the misapprehension that the ball was, in fact, stuck in the ivy. In a frenzy he shook and shook until the ivy trembled but, actually, the ball was resting in plain sight on the ground near his feet.

With the help of his teammates, Heath eventually found the ball but by this time Cavaretta and the two other Cubs who were on base had already crossed home plate.

The Cubs' joy was soon dampened when the umpires ruled that Chicago was entitled to only one run and not three. The decision was based on a ground rule that a batter was entitled to only a double when he hit a ball that went into the Wrigley Field ivy. Spectators responded by hurling all manner of garbage on the field in protest but the umpire's decision held. Nevertheless, Chicago won the game, 5-2.

• • •

When did gnats end a major league baseball game?

On September 15, 1946, the Chicago Cubs were playing the Brooklyn Dodgers in the nightcap of a doubleheader at Ebbets Field, when a swarm of gnats descended on the field in the sixth inning. The gnats irritated the Brooklyn fans, who started waving their white scorecards to ward off the insects. This created a vision hazard for the players, so the Dodgers, leading at the time, were awarded the game.

The Cubs fell victim to another strange phenomenon on May 20, 1960, in Milwaukee, where they were playing the Braves in ever-thickening fog. At the bottom of the fifth, with no score, Umpire Frank Dascoli, working behind the plate, could no longer see the outfielders. Dascoli took his four-man crew to the outfield and had the Cubs' Frank Thomas hit a deliberate fly ball. Neither the umps nor the three Cub outfielders could see the ball. That ended the game, 0-0.

Peculiar events plagued the Pacific Coast League, too,

during the 1940s. One game in Oakland was called because U.S. Cavalrymen on maneuvers had churned up the field. Earthquakes cancelled one game in Seattle, while a total solar eclipse brought a midday game in Ventura, California, to a halt. And when wind blew thick black smoke (from nearby burning trash) over the playing field, a 24-inning tie game in Sacramento came to a choking end.

• • •

George (Moon) Gibson, the marvelous catcher from London, Ontario, was an integral part of one of the world series most unusual three victories. What was Gibson's role?
A catcher for the Pittsburgh Pirates, Gibson was behind the plate when a youngster named Charles (Babe) Adams took the mound against the Detroit Tigers in the 1909 World Series — not once, not twice, but three times.

Paced by fiery Ty Cobb and slugging Wahoo Sam Crawford, the Tigers seemed too powerful for the Pirates. The experts said the only chance Pittsburgh had was a fast curveball pitcher. Manager Fred Clarke of the Pirates had only one such hurler on his staff, Babe Adams. Yet, the Babe was, literally, a babe in the majors. This was his rookie season and the Tigers would be just too much for the kid. Or would they?

Clarke took the gamble and started Adams in the opening game on October 8, 1909. After a nervous opening, Babe settled down and lo and behold he beat Detroit, 4-1.

When Adams was ready to pitch again the series was tied at two games apiece. On October 13 the Babe went to work again and for the second time he beat the Tigers, 8-4. But Detroit rebounded, won Game Six and now the series was deadlocked at three games apiece. The finale was on October 16 and, naturally, Babe Adams was the Pirates' choice.

Now poised and confident, he picked the vaunted Tigers

apart, allowing six hits as his mates walloped the Detroit pitchers. When the dust had cleared the Pirates had won, 8-0, and Babe Adams became the second pitcher to win three games in a best-of-seven series — with a lot of help from Moon Gibson behind the plate!

* * *

In the days of the old Federal League, Grover Lund once hit a 70-foot home run. How did this happen?

One of the umpires failed to show up for a Federal League game in 1914, so the other one, Bill Brennan, stood behind the pitcher in order to both call pitches and see the bases. When hitters started fouling a lot of balls, Brennan called time to stack a huge pile of fresh baseballs behind the pitcher's mount. In that era of baseball history, umpires had no pockets in their uniforms for baseballs.

Grover Lund came up to bat as soon as the stack was precariously perched next to Brennan and proceeded to blast a hard liner into the pile, scattering balls all over the infield. Infielders darted around the field grabbing the first ball they could, while Lund started circling the bases. Lund was tagged with every ball in sight.

Since nobody could prove which ball was the one actually pitched and hit, Brennan ruled that Lund had hit a home run — to the mound!

* * *

Apart from pitching for the Washington Senators and Cleveland Indians, Montreal-born Joe Krakauskas was involved in an unusual episode while playing against the Philadelphia Athletics in the late 1930s. What happened to Joe?

Krakauskas was in the Senators' dugout when one of baseball's biggest brawls erupted on the diamond. While umpire Cal Hubbard scurried around knocking heads together to speed the peacemaking process, Bob Johnson, a

Philadelphia outfielder, stood on the fringe of the melee with a huge smile on his face.

Johnson not only was big, he was tough and, at the time, was one of the most feared ball players, yet he held back as the melee reached its peak — until poor Joe Krakauskas made his unfortunate move.

Krakauskas, who was notorious for his fast, wild pitches, wound up to take a punch at the Athletics' miniscule shortstop, Skeeter Newsome. But before Joe could complete his roundhouse, he felt Johnson's hand grab his shoulder, followed by a fist crashing against his jaw. "Joe dropped like a shot quail," wrote one journalist, "lay still for a moment, then arose and scrambled back to the dugout. Later on he explained that he thought Cal Hubbard had smashed him."

The next day a reporter approached Bob Johnson. "You weren't having any of that fight, Bob," he said, "so why did you clobber poor Joe like that?"

"Because," Johnson answered, "I never could hit that so-and-so when he was pitching!"

• • •

When did rowdy Red Sox fans force a forfeit?

With Sunday curfew rapidly approaching in the second game of a doubleheader between the Red Sox and the Yankees at Boston's Fenway Park, the Yanks scored twice in the top of the eighth to lead 7-5. Twenty minutes remained before curfew would halt the game. If the full inning wasn't completed, the game would merely end in a 5-5 tie.

Yankee players began to take deliberate outs, trying to ensure that the inning would be played. Noting the farce, Red Sox fans showed their disgust by hurling hats, soda bottles, scorecards, peanut shells, hot dog rolls and other assorted debris onto the field. Soon the park was covered with garbage and utterly unplayable. The umpires promptly declared the game a forfeit to the Yankees and added a $1,000 fine to the Sox.

Boston would be the beneficiary later on. Once in Washington, an inept grounds crew failed to cover the field on time during a rain delay. The umpire held that the grounds crew were stalling to protect the Senators' current lead, and gave the game to Boston.

Rowdy fans caused another forfeit, this time to the Texas Rangers, in 1974. It was "Beer Night" in Cleveland, with suds for sale at twenty-five cents a cup. Sure enough chaos soon ensued and the drunken fans stormed the field, ending the game.

In 1980 master promoter Bill Veeck's anti-disco demonstration in Chicago backfired on him. Fans had been asked to bring disco records to Comiskey Park, where they would be destroyed on the field between games of a doubleheader with the Detroit Tigers.

Instead, fans started flinging records on the field and at the end of the game, stormed the field to begin smashing the disks. The beleaguered umpires fined Veeck and awarded the nightcap to the Tigers.

• • •

Name the pitcher who was said to throw a fastball, curve and the biggest shadow in baseball.
Walter "Jumbo" Brown pitched for the New York Yankees and an assortment of other clubs before he completed his career in 1941. Although Brown was not an especially good pitcher he did gain considerable notoriety because of his girth. At 265 pounds, Jumbo was the heaviest player to have ever appeared in the majors up to that time.

Yankees manager Joe McCarthy used Brown sparingly but when he did work it was usually in Philadelphia against the Athletics, who rarely won and who even more infrequently had large crowds at their home field, Shibe Park.

"Why is it you pitch Brown only in Philadelphia?" McCarthy was asked one day.

"It's the only way I know to fill Shibe Park," McCarthy quipped.

In fairness to Brown it should be noted that he won more games than he lost. When he pitched for the Yankees' farm team, the Newark Bears of the International League, in 1934 he became a fan favorite in the New Jersey metropolis. That year Brown led the league in earned run average.

That same year Hy Goldberg of the Newark *Evening News* was asked what sort of stuff Brown threw. "He throws a fastball, curve and the biggest shadow in baseball," Goldberg sallied.

• • •

When did a pitcher argue to have an umpire call one of his pitches a ball rather than a strike?

In the 1930s St. Louis Browns manager Rogers Hornsby had a strict rule that any pitcher who threw one over the plate on a 0-2 count would be slapped with a $50 fine. Hornsby's tactic was to have the pitcher "waste" one in, hopefully goading the batter to swing wildly and strike out.

One day pitcher Jim Walkup had a 0-2 count and his third pitch barely nipped the corner of the plate. The umpire yelled, "strike three."

Walkup stalked off the mound and argued the call desperately, but the umpire stuck to it and Walkup was out $50.

• • •

How did Germany Schaefer once convince an umpire to call a game?

Once in 1908, heavy rain began to disrupt an Indians-Tigers battle. Tiger infielder Germany Schaefer appealed to Umpire Tommy Connolly to call the game. No luck.

Finally Schaefer came out in high rubber boots, raincoat, Gloucester fisherman's hat and umbrella. Connolly stared at Schaefer.

"I have a very bad cold," Schaefer explained, "and it's now bordering on pneumonia. If I get rid of my rubber boots, my raincoat and my umbrella, I will be in the hospital in two hours. And I will certainly sue you and the league."

Connolly called the game.

• • •

How did Wilbert Robinson fool an umpire with a lemon?

In a pre-1900 game between Baltimore and Washington of the National League, umpire Jack Kerns kept the game going in spite of approaching darkness.

Oriole catcher Wilbert Robinson walked to the mound to talk with pitcher John Clarkson. There Robinson slipped Clarkson a lemon and told him to throw it on the next pitch. Clarkson put the baseball in his back pocket, and threw the lemon for the first pitch, as planned.

The umpire called, "strike one." Robinson called time, turned around, and faced the umpire. He opened his glove to show the lemon.

"When you can't tell the difference between a baseball and a lemon, it's time to stop," he said. The embarrassed umpire capitulated.

Even so, most umpires call 'em as they see 'em, even if it goes against the pre-written script. Bill Summers, working on a Hollywood movie set in a cameo role during the off-season, got into a crouch for a scene, and after the pitch whizzed across the plate, called, "strike one!"

The director stopped the shooting and said to Summers, "Bill, that was supposed to be 'ball one.'"

Summers, a veteran umpire, snapped back, "Tell the pitcher I call them as I see them."

• • •

5

QUOTABLE QUOTES

Who said,

1. "Can't anybody here play this game?"
2. "Don't look back; something might be gaining on you."
3. "Going, going, gone."
4. "Good field no hit."
5. "Hit 'em where they ain't."
6. "It's not whether you win or lose but how you play the game."
7. "Nice guys finish last."
8. "Say it ain't so, Joe."

Answers begin on page 172.

Who was the first Blue Jay to win the Rookie of the Year award?

In 1979, Cleveland Indian farmhand castoff Alfredo Griffin was traded to the Jays. He immediately went on an offensive tear, hitting .279, tops among AL shortstops, and set Blue Jay records with hits (179), runs (81), triples (10) and stolen bases (21).

He wound up sharing Rookie of the Year honors with the Twins' John Castino, who hit .285.

• • •

Who hit the first Blue Jay grand slam home run?

On June 27, 1977 Hector Torres hit a grand slam in Toronto's Exhibition Stadium off Yankee hurler Ron Guidry. For the Jays, it was their first grand slam. For Torres, it was the end of a convoluted career in the majors that led him to both Canadian teams.

Torres spent three years as a shortstop in Houston, from 1968 to 1970. He hit no higher than .246, and went to the Cubs in 1971. In 1972, he played for the Expos — where he played second base, third base, shortstop, the outfield . . . and even pitched a game. Posting a sorry 27.00 ERA in only two innings, he fortunately didn't figure in the decision.

When '72 ended, he went on the road again, eventually landing in Toronto, where he hit his record homer in his final season in the majors. Curiously, in 1977, he had a decent season, getting a personal high for home runs with five.

• • •

What pitcher struck out Babe Ruth, Lou Gehrig, Jimmy Foxx, Al Simmons and Joe Cronin in succession during an All-Star game?

"The Meal Ticket," "The Stopper," "King Carl" — all are famous nicknames for the master of the screwball, Carl Hubbell.

Hubbell set a National League record by pitching 46 1/3 consecutive scoreless innings. He won 16 games in a row in 1936 and extended that streak to 24 when he won the first eight games of the 1937 season. He added a no-run, no-hit game against Pittsburgh and an 18-inning game in which he allowed but six hits and no walks. He was the Most Valuable Player twice, in 1933 and again in '36. Yet his performance in one All-Star game was so spectacular that it is this single feat most often remembered when the name Carl Hubbell is recalled.

On July 10, 1934, almost 50,000 fans watched Hubbell pitch for the National League against an "unbeatable" lineup containing nine future Hall of Famers. Hubbell facing down the likes of Ruth, Gehrig and Cronin was a lot like David facing several Goliaths!

The American League clearly was a strong favorite. Despite Charley Gehringer's single (he stole second), and Heinie Manush's walk to first, Hubbell remained calm. Babe Ruth came up. Hubbell released his famous screwball and struck him out. The same fate awaited Lou Gehrig, Jimmy Foxx, Al Simmons and Joe Cronin. Bill Dickey succeeded in hitting a lowly single, upsetting Hubbell's streak.

But the American League won anyway 9-7. Hubbell did not even figure in the decision. Instead Mel Harder was credited with defeating Van Lingle Mungo.

• • •

Name the player who dashed from first to home on a single, scoring the run needed to win that year's series. During the fifth game of the 1946 World Series, Enos (Country) Slaughter was slammed in the right elbow by a pitched ball from Joe Dobson of the Boston Red Sox. Typical of Slaughter, he ignored both the swollen elbow and Doc Hyland's suggestion not to play. When the Cardinals and the Red Sox met in St. Louis to play the sixth game, Enos was in the line-up.

After the Cards won the game, 4-1, the series was tied at three games apiece. In the finale, the Red Sox scored first — Wally Moses and Johnny Pesky both singled, with Dom DiMaggio's fly bringing in Moses. The score was tied in the second on Whitey Kurowski's double, an infield out, and Harry Walker's fly.

The Cards then took a 3-1 lead in the fifth. But in the eighth, with Card pitcher Murray Dickson out and David Brecheen in, two runs scored on a DiMaggio double, tying the score at 3-3.

In the bottom of the eighth, Enos managed his soon-to-be fateful single, followed by Whitey Kurowski and Del Rice, who both flied out. Harry Walker was up next and Slaughter was becoming anxious to run. Eddie Dyer, the St. Louis manager, gave Enos the sign to move on the pitch. Walker hit a line drive into center as Enos took off from first. Slaughter watched outfielder Leon Culberson fumble and tore on to third. Mike Gonzalez was there directing traffic, but to Enos, Gonzalez might as well have been invisible. With no hesitation, Slaughter whipped around the bases and headed for home.

A mighty throw from unsuspecting shortstop Johnny Pesky to home brought the Boston catcher, Hal Wagner, far up the third base line. Slaughter slid right over the plate scoring the run the Cardinals needed to earn their sixth world championship and make Brecheen only the seventh pitcher to win three games in one series.

● ● ●

What team scored ten hits to overcome an 8-0 deficit and win a World Series game?

It was the 1929 Series between the Cubs and the A's. The Chicago Cubs had a "seemingly insurmountable" lead of 8-0 in the fourth game. At the end of six and a half innings, there appeared little hope for the Philadelphia Athletics.

It was a sluggish game for the A's — they had only three hits in the first six innings when Al Simmons slammed in a homer in the bottom of the seventh. An 8-1 score seemed hardly less dismal. After Simmons, Jimmy Foxx singled, followed by Bing Miller, Jimmy Dykes and Joe Boley. The A's were now behind 8-3. Another run batted in by Max Bishop brought the score to 8-4.

Cub pitcher Charlie Root was removed. Phillie's Mule Haas line-drived to right, a fly ball that ordinarily would have been caught. In the field, Hack Wilson came for the ball, was blocked by the sun in his eyes, and ducked away. The ball bounced out into deep center as Haas raced behind two fellow players for an inside-the-park home run. The A's were only one run behind.

Mickey Cochrane walked, and Cub pitcher Art Nehf was replaced with Sheriff Blake. Al Simmons smacked in his second hit of the inning with a single, followed by Foxx as Cochrane scored. It was 8-8.

Joe McCarthy, the frantic Cub manager, put in Pat Malone, who hit Miller with a frantic pitch, loading the bases. A line drive to left field from Jimmy Dykes slipped out of outfielder Stephenson's fingers, sending Dykes to second and two more players home. The A's had scored 10 runs from 10 hits. The final score — 10-8.

• • •

Do you remember when the Brooklyn Dodgers had three runners on one base?

On August 15, 1928, Dodger slugger Babe Herman ripped a pitch toward the right field fence with one out and the bases loaded. The ball looped short of the fence, and the runner waited to see if it would be caught. Meanwhile, Herman started running.

The ball dropped and the runner on third scored. Behind him, Dazzy Vance ran from second, and slowed down as he rounded third. Chick Fewster, behind Vance, followed. Herman followed both of them.

The Dodger third base coach, Mickey O'Neil, aware that Vance wouldn't score on the relay, yelled, "Back! Back!"

Vance turned around and slid into third, from the home-plate side. Fewster, behind Vance, hopped on the bag. Herman, coming in from second, slid in as well.

Third baseman Eddie Taylor caught the relay, and tagged all three base runners. The umpire called Fewster and Herman out, ending the inning.

Dodger manager Wilbert Robinson was beside himself, but it probably wasn't as bad as the time Herman stole second while runners were on second and third.

• • •

How did the Blue Jays get their name?
When expansion to Toronto was approved by the American League, in March, 1976, the Jays' owner held a "name the team" contest.

30,000 entries suggesting over 4,000 names were sent in. From the list of names submitted, a panel of judges chose the name "Blue Jays" from the list. 154 people had submitted the name "Blue Jays," so a draw was held to determine the grand prize winner.

He turned out to be Dr. William Mills, of Etobicoke, Ontario. Dr. Mills won an all-expense paid trip to Dunedin, Florida, to the Jays' first spring training.

• • •

Who was the first Blue Jay pitcher to win an All-Star game?
From 1971 to 1982, the National League dominated the mid-summer classic, but in 1983, the AL exploded behind Fred Lynn's record-setting grand slam. The beneficiary of the AL power display in Chicago's Comiskey Park was Dave Stieb, of the Toronto Blue Jays, who started the game.

• • •

Dizzy Dean once took back a home run he hit. How did he do that?

When Dizzy Dean was pitching in the minors at Houston, he hit a rare home run. Immediately afterward he lost his control and walked three batters in a row. The Houston manager yanked Dean.

Upset, Dean ran to the scoreboard and tore down the numeral "1" that represented his home run. With the painted wooden square in his hands, he marched off the field to the clubhouse, where his manager demanded to know why Dean had taken the sign.

Quipped Dean, "If I can't pitch, you can't have my run."

• • •

The Orioles and Yankees once engineered a 17-player trade. Can you recall the participants?

At the end of the 1954 season, Yankee general manager George Weiss, annoyed at his team's failure to win the pennant despite winning 104 games, launched a huge swap with the Baltimore Orioles. Baltimore got nine players: pitcher Harry Boyd, Jim McDonald and Bill Miller; catchers Gus Triandos and Hal Smith; second baseman Don Leppert; third baseman Kal Segrist; shortstop Willie Miranda; and outfielder Gene Woodling.

The Yankees received pitchers Don Larsen, Bob Turley and Mike Blyzka; catcher Darrell Johnson; first baseman Dick Kryhoski; shortstop Billy Hunter; and outfielders Ted Del Guercio and Jim Fridley.

Larsen and Turley would be key men for the Yanks, as they went on to pitch the Yankees to four pennants.

• • •

What was the "Williams Shift?"

Ted Williams enjoyed great success against Lou Boudreau's Cleveland Indians until 1946, when Boudreau, the shortstop-manager, came up with a tactic to deflate Williams' batting average.

On July 14, 1946, after Williams had hit three homers including a grand slam in the opener of a doubleheader,

1. With a break or two, Toronto-born Goody Rosen could have won a National League batting championship for the Brooklyn Dodgers. He didn't but he remained a favorite of the Ebbets Field faithful (shown here in the background).

2. Almost killed in World War II, Phil Marchildon, who hailed from Penetanguishene, Ontario, returned to the pitching wars to star for the Philadelphia Athletics in the late 1940s.

3. There was only one "Twinkle-Toes" in baseball history. His true monicker was George Selkirk. He hailed from Huntsville, Ontario and starred for the New York Yankees.

4. Only one first-baseman could ever claim to have lulled an infant to sleep with a lullaby in the Brooklyn Dodgers' club car enroute to Pittsburgh. That man was the Brooks' tenor-infielder John Buddy Hassett.

5. This manager, temporarily-turned-golfer, Gene Mauch, was named National League Manager-of-the-Year in 1973 as pilot of the Montreal Expos.

WIDE WORLD PHOTOS

6. The best pitcher ever to come out of Chatham, Ontario was Ferguson Jenkins, shown here winding up to toss one for the Chicago Cubs.

7. Ron LeFlore, discovered by Billy Martin at a Michigan penitentiary, signed and played with the Detroit Tigers (1974-79) and the Montreal Expos (1980) before ending his career with the Chicago Cubs (1981-82).

8. Andre (The Hawk) Dawson, Rookie-of-the-Year winner in 1977 (Montreal Expos), is considered a superstar by many, but has yet to win the MVP award.

Boudreau unveiled his move. He had six fielders stationed on the right side of the diamond — where the lefthanded Williams got most of his hits — with the left fielder, playing deep shortstop, the only man on the left side of the infield.

Williams, a student of hitting, could have overcome the shift by bunting or slicing the ball to the opposite field, but that would have reduced his power — which was Boudreau's aim. Williams decided to take on the shift directly.

At first Williams was amazed. He later said, "I had to laugh when I saw it." But then he realized they were robbing him of his power. Williams tried to fight the shift by challenging the defense. Inevitably, his average dropped.

But on September 13, 1946, in Cleveland again, Williams paid Boudreau back for the shift. With the shift still on, Williams hit a line drive deep to left center field, which rolled to the wall. Center fielder Pat Seerey ran it down, and Williams ran around the bases to pick up the only inside-the-park home run of his career. It won the ball game, 1-0.

• • •

Who served up Pete Rose's National League record-breaking 3,631st hit?

Pete Rose's quest to surpass Stan Musial as the top hit man in National League history was temporarily halted by the baseball strike in June, July and August, 1981. When the season resumed on August 10th, Rose had 3,630 hits, tying him with Stan Musial for number one.

In the post-strike "opener," Rose's Philadelphia Phillies hosted the St. Louis Cardinals. In the seventh inning, Rose connected for a single to right field off reliever Mark Littell, for hit number 3,631.

The game was halted for a brief ceremony, in which Rose was given the ball, and congratulated by the man whose record he had broken, Stan Musial.

Littell would go down in history like many other pitchers as a man who had served up famous hits. In fact, he served up two. In 1976, he was with the Kansas City Royals, and in the final game of the American League playoffs, he fired a pitch to the Yankees' Chris Chambliss that was hit over the fence for the pennant-winning home run . . . the first Yankee pennant since 1964.

Interestingly, Littell did not figure in the decision in the Rose game in 1981. The game had been lost by a Card pitcher earlier.

• • •

Who was the first manager of Expos?
Gene Mauch led the Expos in their first season, 1969. Mauch had a reputation as a brilliant tactician, but he never managed a World Series.

Branch Rickey said of him, "You look at this boy and you think he's 16. You talk to him and you think he's 26. You talk baseball with him and you think he's 36."

As a bench-warmer in the '40s and '50s with a variety of teams, he would forever ask his managers about their tactics.

"One day with the Dodgers," he recalled, "I walked into Durocher's office and said, 'This isn't a second-guess. I'd just like to know why you hit-and-run in the third inning. With Stanky on first and Pee Wee Reese up, it looked to me like a bunt situation.' "

"Durocher said to me, 'Kid, people talk about percentages. I got my own percentages.' "

In 1953, Mauch started managing, first in the Pacific Coast League, then with the Minneapolis Millers. In 1960 he became manager of the Phillies. In 1969 he took over the Expos for their first year.

• • •

A Canadian set the record for the most saves in a single season! Can you name him?
John Hiller, born in Toronto, set a major league record in

1973, with 38 saves for the Detroit Tigers.

Hiller was also a key man in the Tigers' 1968 and 1972 pennant drives. But what made his saves so much more impressive was that in 1971 Hiller had open-heart surgery, then came back to win the Comeback Player of the Year Award in 1973. He retired in 1981, due to a recurrence of the heart trouble.

Hiller's record held up for ten years, until Dan Quisenberry of the Kansas City Royals saved 43 games in 1983, establishing a new record.

• • •

Can you recall the first French-Canadian to win a major league game in Montreal?
When Claude (Frenchy) Raymond came out of the bullpen on May 16, 1969, in Montreal's Jarry Park, he was met with a standing ovation, even though he was a member of the opposing team, the Atlanta Braves.

"I had tears in my eyes that night," Raymond recalled. "I was so nervous I dropped the ball thrown back from the catcher!"

The last time Raymond had played in Jarry Park, it had been as an amateur and the seating capacity had been only 20,000. But on this May day, the refurbished ballpark held 28,000 fans who watched Raymond win for the Braves, 7-5.

A few months later Raymond was bought by the Montreal Expos on waivers. He went on to become the first Canadian player on Canada's first major league team, thus becoming the first French-Canadian to win *in* Canada, and the first to win *for* Canada.

• • •

Who gave up Babe Ruth's final home runs in major league play?
When Guy Bush of the Pittsburgh Pirates strutted out to

the mound on May 24, 1935, he relieved Guy Lucas, who had earlier in the game given up Babe Ruth's 712th career home run.

Bush was no fan of the Bambino, who was playing out his final season as a Boston Brave. Indeed, Bush hated all batters.

"I wanted no part of any of them, Ruth included," Bush recalled. "I never spoke to an opposing player for the ten years I played in the major leagues except to shout at 'em from the top step of the dugout."

The book on Ruth was to keep the ball moving around the plate — and try to get lucky. First time up against Bush, Ruth struck out swinging. This led Bush to believe that Ruth, at age 40, had a blind spot. Bush threw that same pitch when Ruth next came to bat and the Babe hit a scorching drive that "nearly killed my second baseman," Bush said.

Next time up, Bush eased a slow curve. Babe hit it down the right field line, 20 feet into the stands for his second homer of the day, and 713th career shot.

Bush felt insulted and called his catcher, Tommy Padden, to the mount. "Tommy," said Bush, "I don't think the Big Bamboo can hit my fastball." Bush didn't think that Ruth, standing at the plate with his back practically to the mound, could come around fast enough to whip the fastball.

Bush asked Padden to notify the Sultan of Swat that a fastball was on the way!

"In fact, I told Tommy to go back and *tell* the Big Bamboo what I was going to do; that I was going to damn him to hit my fastball. That's how confident I was.

"I threw two fastballs and he hit the second one for the longest ball I ever saw."

It would be one of the longest home runs *anybody* ever saw. It cleared Forbes Field, the first homer ever to do so, and landed on a construction lot, where one Henry Diorio retrieved it. He later took the ball to the Braves' hotel and had it autographed by the Babe, who noted that, as far as he was concerned, it was just another home run.

But it wasn't. It was the first time three were hit in one day by one man in Pittsburgh, and it would be Ruth's 714th and final home run, a record that would stand for 39 years.

• • •

Who was the last Brooklyn Dodger to play in the majors?

It's appropriate that the last man to play for the Brooklyn Dodgers and retire from the game was a Brooklyn native, Bob Aspromonte.

In 1956, Aspromonte was sent up to pinch-hit for Brooklyn in a late-season game. After grounding out, Aspromonte was sent to the minors, and came back in 1960 with the Dodgers, now in Los Angeles.

He then went to the Houston Astros, where he played a variety of infield positions, and then to the Braves in 1969, finishing up in 1971 with the New York Mets as a third baseman. Aspromonte's best year was 1967, when he hit .294, with six home runs.

Incidentally, the last active New York Giant was a slightly more famous ballplayer, and he, too, finished his career with the Mets. Willie Mays.

• • •

How did a catcher cost the Phillies $10,000 by not thinking?

On June 8, 1947, the Pirates and Phillies were tied in Philadelphia at 4-4 in the eighth inning. Then, in the top of the ninth, Pirate Ralph Kiner hit a home run.

It was nearly 7 pm and there was an early curfew in Philadelphia. If the game did not end by 7 o'clock, the score reverted to the last complete inning. If there was a tie, the game would be replayed the next day as part of a doubleheader.

Both the Pirates and the Phillies were aware of this. The Pirates had little desire to play a doubleheader, but the Phillies wanted the extra $10,000 in admission tickets a doubleheader would bring. In order to hasten the outcome of the game, Pirates' Hank Greenberg allowed himself to be out.

When the Phillies came up, Manager Ben Chapman told his men to delay as much as possible. The first man popped out. The second man, Charley Gilbert, a pinch-hitter, took an excessively long time to select a bat. Then he argued with umpire Babe Pinelli, intentionally fouled off some pitches and finally struck out. One more out and the Phillies would lose both the game and the $10,000 gate money from a doubleheader.

Chapman called for second-string catcher Hugh Poland, stationed 300 feet away in the bullpen, to hit, anticipating that Poland would take some time to come in, eating up the clock.

Much to Chapman's dismay, Poland ran in without realizing that the purpose of his appearance was to delay the game.

When Poland arrived, he saw that he had to counteract his dash. He argued briefly with Umpire Pinelli, but Pinelli hurried him back to the box.

Poland took two strikes and then hit a lazy fly ball, which Pirate Wally Westlake caught — 52 seconds before curfew. The Phillies lost the game — and the $10,000.

• • •

How did Dizzy Dean make a comeback for the Browns?
By 1938, Dizzy Dean had seen his best pitches go by. In the 1930s, he'd been the best pitcher baseball had ever seen. Then the St. Louis Cardinals traded him to the Cubs, where he just couldn't do a thing. Worst of all, his fastball was gone. After two years with the Cubs, Dizzy was forced down to the minor leagues. Even with Tulsa in the Texas League, the best he could do was break even. When the St.

Louis Browns asked him to become their radio broadcaster, Dizzy gladly accepted. He knew he just couldn't play any longer.

The only problem Dizzy had with broadcasting was that he usually talked about himself. Dizzy was told to instead talk about the good plays the Browns were making, and the Browns' pitching staff. One day, Dizzy became so disgusted with the Browns that he blurted out over the radio, "Whatsa' matter with these guys? Their fastballs wouldn't break a pane of glass. Doggone if I know what this game's comin' to. I'll bet I could beat nine out of ten of these guys that call themselves pitchers these days."

Many of the pitchers' wives happened to be listening to the broadcast and became furious. They began calling President DeWitt of the Browns, complaining about Dizzy, even challenging him to prove his grand statement. DeWitt decided that he could use the increased attendance at a Brown game, as they were attracting small crowds during their slump. DeWitt invited Dizzy to pitch a game for the Browns. Dizzy agreed and attendance for the game rose from the usual 2,000 to 16,000.

The first batter Dizzy faced was Don Kolloway, the White Sox' first baseman. Kolloway singled into the outfield. The next batter hit into a double play and the third grounded out. Dean had come through the first inning unscathed. In the second, Dean allowed a single and a walk with one out. By this point, it appeared as if Dizzy had been incorrect in his assessment of his abilities compared to the other Browns pitchers. But Dizzy had a few good pitches left. The next batter hit into a double play, ending the inning. When Dizzy came to bat, he hit a line drive into left field, but pulled a muscle in his leg on the way to first base. Although Dizzy tried to cover up his injury, it was apparent when he stepped to the mound in the fourth inning that his leg was giving him trouble. The first batter hit a single, but Dizzy got rid of the next three pretty quickly. Dizzy knew when he walked off the mound in the fourth inning that he had pitched his last game. His leg was hurting him too much to continue playing.

Dizzy had proven his point anyway. Facing only fourteen batters in four innings, he had held the White Sox in check. Unfortunately, a relief pitcher lost the game in the ninth inning. But the defeat was not at all related to Dizzy's performance.

Dizzy summed up his feelings to a journalist the next day. "I said I could pitch as good as most of these fellers," Dean commented, "and I can. But I'll be doggoned if I'm ever gonna try again. Talking's my game now, and I'm just glad that the muscle I pulled wasn't in my throat."

• • •

Prior to 1884 pitchers used a special delivery to home plate. What was so special about it?
They threw underhanded.

• • •

What was the unusual strategem that brought Walter Johnson to the majors?
Walter Johnson, the famed "Big Train," who until 1983 held the all-time record for strikeouts, was burning up the amateur leagues in Idaho in 1906. Somehow, word of young Johnson reached the manager of the Washington Senators' Joe Cantillon.

Cantillon tried to ignore the reports, busy with a last-place team, but finally he became fed up and sent Cliff Blankenship, a catcher on the injured list, to Weiser, Idaho to see the young man the letters described as "the greatest pitcher in baseball."

"Bring your bat with you," Cantillon told Blankenship. "If you get even a loud foul off him, leave him there."

A few days later, Cantillon got a telegram from Blankenship. "You can't hit what you can't see. I've signed him and he's leaving today."

And until 1927, nobody else could hit Walter Johnson, either.

• • •

Can you recall the very first lineup the Expos had?
On April 8, 1969, baseball became an international sport when the Montreal Expos opened the season in New York, facing the Mets. Canada had made the bigs.

The lineup was as follows:

Maury Wills, shortstop
Gary Sutherland, second base
Rusty Staub, right field
Mack Jones, left field
Bob Bailey, first base
John Bateman, catcher
Coco Laboy, third base
Don Hahn, center field
Mudcat Grant, pitcher

The players were a varied lot. Wills was at the tail end of a stellar career, which included 2,000 hits and 586 stolen bases. In 1962, with the Dodgers, he stole a record 104 sacks. But he only lasted 47 games with the Expos, hitting .222 before he was dispatched to Los Angeles.

Sutherland came to the Expos from the Phillies, where he had been a utility player. In 1969, he was the Expos' second baseman all year. He hit only .239, and didn't improve much before 1972, when he went to Houston.

Staub turned out to be Montreal's trump card until 1972. In 1969, he hit 29 homers, batted .302 and drove in 79 men. In 1970 he hit 30 homers, and added a .311 average in 1971. In 1972, he was traded to the Mets. Staub returned to the Expos briefly in 1979 as a pinch-hitter.

Cleanup hitter Mack Jones was also at the tag end of a career that encompassed four cities. With the Braves he hit 31 homers in 1965, earning the sobriquet "Mack The Knife." With the Expos, he hit 22 homers in 1969, drove in

79, with a .270 clip. After that he lost his effectiveness, hitting .240 and .165, before retiring at the end of 1971.

Bob Bailey hit the ball well for the Expos, crossing the 20-home-run mark thrice in his seven-year tour with Montreal. He played third base, the outfield and first base. In 1969, he had a .265 average, 9 homers and 53 RBIs.

John Bateman would not be the regular catcher for Montreal in '69. Ron Brand got that unhappy chore and with good reason. Bateman hit a mere .209 while Brand hit .258. Bateman had been a good-field, no-hit catcher with Houston for five years, and continued to catch for the Expos until mid-1972, when he was traded to the Phillies.

Coco Laboy was a minor-league outfielder who made it to the Expos after ten years by switching to third base. In 1969, he hit 18 homers, with a .258 average. After that, National league pitchers found his weaknesses, and he lost his power. His fielding average at third wasn't too good, either. In 1973, he retired from the Expos, with a .233 lifetime average.

Don Hahn only played four games for the Expos in 1969. He got one hit. After he left for the minors, Adolfo Phillips took over in center field, in mid-season. He was no improvement. He hit .216.

Mudcat Grant was also at the end of the line, and after 11 games with the Expos — with a 1-6 record — he was shipped to St. Louis. Grant's best year had been 1965, when he won 21 games for Minnesota Twins, to lead the American League.

The Expos won their opener, and then lost 110 more games after that. The initial game was an 11-10 thriller, though, in which Laboy, Staub and Dan McGinn homered for the Expos. Don Shaw won the game in relief, defeating Met reliever Cal Koonce.

• • •

Which Montreal Expo set the record for most pinch-hits?

In 1976, Jose Morales set a number of pinch-hitting records with the Expos, including most games as a pinch-hitter, 82; most at-bats as a pinch-hitter, 78; most pinch-hits, 25; and most RBIs as a pinch-hitter, 24.

He hit .316, and actually played some games without pinch-hitting — as a backup first baseman-catcher. He led the National League twice in pinch-hits, and the AL twice.

• • •

In 1908, when the famed "Tinker-Evers-Chance" poem was written, how many double plays did the combination actually make?
Columnist Franklin P. Adams wrote his renowned poem about the Chicago Cubs' infield:

These are the saddest of possible words:
  "Tinker to Evers to Chance."
Trio of bear Cubs and fleeter than birds,
  "Tinker to Evers to Chance"
Ruthlessly pricking our gonfalon bubble,
Turning a Giant hit into a double —
Words that are heavy with nothing but trouble:
  "Tinker to Evers to Chance."

The infield consisted of Harry Steinfeldt at third base, Joe Tinker at shortstop, Johnny Evers at second and Frank Chance at first.

The combination was hard-hitting and fielded well, but in their 1908 World Championship season, made only eight double plays.

They must have all been clutch plays!

• • •

When did a private citizen try to buy a major league ballplayer . . . for one dollar?
When Dick Stuart, hard-hitting and poor-fielding first baseman, was released by the Mets, Marvin Kitman, of Leonia, New Jersey, discovered he could buy the slugger's contract for one dollar. Kitman figured that Stuart could

teach his young son the nuances of batting for the kid's Little League ball.

Kitman wrote to Stuart, "I've decided to pick up your contract for 1967." Kitman included a personal check for one dollar.

Kitman went on to write that Stuart's job was "to teach my boy the fundamentals of the game, especially fielding." He added that Stuart could teach young Kitman how to sign a money-making contract when young Kitman made the majors.

The letter concluded by expressing the hope that the two men would work out a fair price for Stuart's services for 1967, and asked what size shirt (emblazoned with the symbol of the Kitman boy's little league team) Stuart needed.

A few days later, Dick Stuart called Kitman, and asked how much money Kitman had in mind. Kitman talked about Branch Rickey's ethics, about hungry ballplayers and deferred payments for Stuart when young Kitman signed with the majors.

Stuart pointed out that he made $40,000 in 1965. Kitman decided to try leasing Stuart on a day-to-day basis to other fathers who needed coaches for their sons. He had two dads lined up when Stuart signed with the Los Angeles Dodgers.

Wrote Kitman to Stuart, in one last try, "Just a reminder that my offer still holds for next season. Spring training begins on April 1 at Sylvan Park in Leonia. I don't want to influence your decision, but Sylvan Park has a short left-field wall."

●　　●　　●

How did Hall-of-Fame umpire Jocko Conlan start his career?

During a doubleheader in St. Louis in 1935, Jocko Conlan, then a White Sox player, broke his thumb and had to be sidelined. Meanwhile, one of the two umpires assigned to the game passed out in the 114° heat. Conlan, idle, volunteered to umpire. He didn't know why. Manager Jimmie Dykes let him, White Sox uniform and all.

Conlan was sent to cover the bases. When Sox shortstop Luke Appling ripped a triple, Conlan ran along, exhorting Appling. But the St. Louis Browns had Appling easily, and Conlan called him out.

Jimmie Dykes ran up to Conlan screaming. "What do you mean, he's out! He's not out! He's safe!" Dykes yelled.

"He's out," Conlan said.

Dykes yelled, "The man was safe."

Appling, slowly getting up from the dirt, said, "No, Papa Dykes. He's right. He had me. He just got me."

"He missed you," Dykes insisted.

"He didn't miss him," Conlan said. "I called him out, and he's out."

Dykes threw himself up, put a hurt look on his face, and said to Conlan, "You're a fine guy to have on a ball club," and walked away.

A few days later, Conlan, at the end of his playing career, started his umpiring career.

• • •

What were Heinie Zimmerman's problems with getting his pay?

When Chicago Cub third baseman Heinie Zimmerman was in the minors, he had played just six weeks when the club owner summoned the players to say, "Boys, the club is bankrupt. But don't worry, I'll pay off right now in alphabetical order." When the owner reached the J's, he was out of money. Zimmerman had to bum a ride home.

The owner's finances improved a month later and he called back his players. Zimmerman showed up. The owner looked at his list, and said, "You're Zimmerman with a Z, aren't you?"

"Not even close," shot back Zimmerman. "I'm Adams, with an A."

• • •

6

1. How many times did Canadian-born pitcher Ferguson Jenkins win 20 games?
2. Can you name the two Canadian pitchers who were original Mets?
3. Who was the first Canadian to lose a World Series game?
4. Who was the first Canadian pitcher to *lose* 20 games?
5. Which current Blue Jay was a member of the original 1969 Kansas City Royals?
6. One of the worst trades the Expos engineered sent Ken Singleton and Mike Torrez to the Baltimore Orioles. Whom did they get in return?
7. Who replaced Gene Mauch when he was fired as manager of the Expos?
8. Name the original Blue Jay who homered in his only World Series at-bat.
9. The Blue Jays' pitching coach posted a 1-12 record with the 1962 New York Mets, winning his only game on the season's finale. Who was he?
10. The Blue Jays' first hero hit two homers on opening day, 1977. Who was he?

Answers begin on page 172.

The 1962 New York Mets set a record for most defeats in a season with 120. Which team did they surpass in their record-breaking season of futility?

The 1916 Philadelphia A's set the record for ignominy with 117 defeats, under the leadership of the great Connie Mack.

All of Mack's wiles were insufficient to help a club that had been decimated the year before when its star players jumped to the outlaw Federal League. Thus the team that had garnered four pennants since 1910 finished 54 1/2 games off the pace in September of 1916.

In the 1950s, former A's pitcher Tom Sheehan, then a scout for the San Francisco Giants, recalled the club at a dinner.

"We lost 20 in a row at one point that summer and I had a haunting feeling we'd never win another. We lost 19 straight on the road. In one game our pitchers gave up 18 walks and in another we left 17 men on base, though I don't know how that many guys got on in the first place."

Some of the men masquerading as ballplayers on this team included Hall-of-Famer Napoleon Lajoie, struggling through his final year at age 41; and rookie Whitey Witt, who made 70 errors at shortstop.

The first baseman was stalwart Stuffy McInnis, who hit .295 but "the third baseman was new every day. Connie Mack must have recruited them from the stands. Some of them didn't stay around long enough to be introduced." One, Charlie Pick by name, made 41 errors.

"Wally Schang, the old catcher, was in left field, and a kid named Lee King hit .188 in right. Billy Meyer (hitting .232) caught half a season until he got appendicitis in May.

"After he left, everybody caught. Remember Val Picinich? He was 19 — he hit .195. On other days, total strangers would catch.

"Once we were playing the Yankees at the Polo Grounds and I'm pitching. Picinich warms me up, but as the first

103

hitter gets in, Val goes back to the bench and takes off the tools.

"Another guy comes out, a guy I've never seen. He comes out to the mound and says, 'My name is Carroll. I'm the catcher. What are your signs?' I tell him not to confuse me and get the heck back there and catch. He stuck around for about a week and nobody ever saw him again." The unfortunate Ralph Carroll caught ten games and hit .091.

The pitchers had a rough time, too. "Once we go to Boston for a series. I pitch the opener (of a doubleheader) and give up one hit. But it happens to follow a walk and an error by Witt, and I lose, 1-0.

"Now Johnnie Nabors pitches the second game and he is leading, 1-0, going into the ninth. He gets the first man. Witt boots one and the next guy walks. Hooper is up next, I think, and he singles to left and the man on second tries to score. Well, Schang has a good arm (in left) and he throws one in that has the runner cold by 15 feet. But we have one of those green catchers. (A fellow named Mike Murphy.) The ball bounces out of his glove, the run scores, the other runner takes third and it is 1-1.

"Nabor winds up and throws the next pitch 20 feet over the hitter's head into the grandstand, the man on third scores and we lose another, 2-1.

"Later I asked Nabors why he threw that one away.

"'Look,' he said, 'I knew those guys wouldn't get me another run and if you think I'm going to throw nine more innings on a hot day like this, you're crazy.'"

And Sheehan himself? He pitched in 38 games with a sparkling 1-15 record.

• • •

Who scored from third on Bobby Thomson's famous "miracle" home run?

On October 3, 1951, during the ninth inning of the final playoff game between the Brooklyn Dodgers and the New

York Giants, New York's Don Mueller slid into third base, twisting and injuring his ankles. Manager Leo Durocher immediately summoned a pinch-runner to replace him, in the form of Clint Hartung, a utility outfielder.

Hartung, a huge, big-eared, ungainly looking fellow, had been trumpeted in 1945 as the Giants' new superstar. The Giants' hopes came to naught; Hartung was neither an effective hitter nor a strong pitcher. By 1951, he was a relic on the Giants, a reminder of their earlier days as a team loaded with huge, muscular power hitters.

But the 1951 club, featuring Alvin Dark, Eddie Stanky, and a rookie named Willie Mays, was a team built more on speed, pitching and defense than on pure stroking power.

Thus, when Bobby Thomson stepped up to the plate, Hartung was down at third, Whitey Lockman stood on second, and the Giants were down, 4-2. Thomson hit Dodger relief pitcher Ralph Branca's second pitched into the left field stands to win the pennant, and Hartung chugged home.

Why was Hartung sent in? Manager Leo Durocher, on the third base coaching lines, had been getting on the Dodgers and pitcher Don Newcombe all day. Before Newcombe was relieved, Durocher placed Hartung at third, so that he had a bruiser between himself and the angry Dodger bench, which made threats to Durocher when the game was over.

As it turned out, Hartung's brawn was unnecessary. The Giants won.

* * *

Sportswriter George Phair summed up the mathematics of the pennant race very clearly and simply in the Old *New York American*. Can you remember how he did it?
In a poem, Phair wrote:

If the Giants win but two of four
And the Dodgers six of ten
The Phillies, as in days of yore,

Will finish last again.
Which just about sums it up!

* * *

Babe Pinelli was the first umpire to call a forfeit of a big league game short of legal length. What led to this bizarre event?

One night Pinelli was reading a menu with his glasses on, when St. Louis Cardinal manager Eddie Stanky came in.

"Well, it's old Horn Rims," he snapped, loudly, "I always said you were blind as a potato with a thousand eyes."

Several days later, Stanky's club was down 8-1, in a game with the Phillies, in the top of the fifth. Stanky tried stalling until darkness to force a postponement.

He pulled delay after delay, running pitchers in and out, complaining on every pitch. Then he had his catcher, Sal Yvars, start a phony fight. Finally Pinelli had had enough.

He turned to Stanky and said, "Well, I won't need glasses to read the papers tonight," and signalled a forfeit.

Stanky never again questioned Pinelli's eyesight.

* * *

A third baseman once started a triple play by literally using his head! How did this come about?

Joe Cronin once ripped a liner with the bases loaded and no outs that came in shoulder-high on third baseman Sammy Hale. Hale couldn't get his glove up in time and all the runners were moving.

The ball bounced off Hale's forehead and carommed gently on the fly to shortstop Billy Knickerbocker's glove for one out. Knickerbocker fired to second, and the ball went around the horn for the second and third outs. Hale was the fourth out of the inning — out cold.

* * *

Name the two pitching brothers who, together, own the

most major league victories in regular-season play and who are the runners-up?

The Perry Brothers, Gaylord and Jim, between them accumulated 529 wins through the 1983 season. The next two brothers have a combined total of 373 victories — but unexpectedly they are not the Dean boys, though Dizzy and Daffy did manage to garner exactly 200 wins between them during their major league career. The second winningest brother combination? It is the Mathewsons, Christy and Henry, who registered their second-place total of 373 while with the New York Giants in the early 1900s. There's just one small catch. Christy won *all* of those games! Henry Mathewson pitched for the Giants in 1906 and 1907, appeared in three games and had one decision, a loss. Not much of a contributor, was he?

• • •

Which batter broke up a perfect game with two out in the ninth inning?

In 1932, Dave (Sheriff) Harris, an outfielder for the Washington Senators, singled with two out in the ninth to rob Detroit Tigers' pitcher Tommy Bridges of a perfect game. There have only been 12 perfect games pitched in the history of the major leagues. Incidentally, Dave Harris was indeed a genuine sheriff, serving the community of Greensboro, South Carolina.

• • •

A Brooklyn Dodger launched the post-World War II baseball player revolution in this country. Who was he?

Luis Francisco Rodriguez Olmo was the player who jumped to the Mexican League from the Dodgers. It all happened immediately after World War II when big leaguers wanted minimum salaries of $5,000 a year, shorter spring training schedules and a limit on salary cuts. Those who were discontented looked to the Mexican League, in the manner that American pro football players now find an alternative in Canada. Defectors such as Olmo drew three-year suspensions, and, soon after his return to Brooklyn, Olmo was shipped to the Boston Braves. Before leaving Brooklyn, Luis played with the Dodgers in the 1949 World Series and hit a home run. Today, Olmo is playing "the best golf of my life." Some of the professionals in Puerto Rico, where he lives, believe he could have been a pro golf star if he had started playing golf instead of baseball in his teens.

• • •

Which tempestuous catcher owned the nickname "Scrap Iron?"

Clint Courtney, a major leaguer for 10 years was dubbed Scrap Iron by his teammates while playing for the St. Louis Browns in 1952. It was during spring training that Courtney bet New York *Mirror* writer Arthur Richman (now assistant to the General Manager for the New York Mets) $100 on a foot race between the two. The challenge took place at a railroad station in Colton, California with the roadbed as the track. The race was won by Richman in a convincing manner, but Courtney claimed the newsman bumped him and requested and got a rematch. The results of the second race were the same, except that at the finish line Courtney tripped and dived head first into the cinderstrewn race course. Courtney was a mess. His clothes were torn to shreds and his body cut all over. It took the trainer well over an hour to treat Courtney's wounds. At breakfast the next morning, Browns' manager Rogers Hornsby, who had not witnessed the race, looked up at Courtney and asked, "What the hell happened to you?"

"I was in a race," replied Courtney, who closely resembled a mutilated mummy.

"How did you do?" asked Hornsby.

"I lost," answered Courtney, grimacing with every syllable.

"Okay," said Hornsby. "It will either be a $250 fine or you can catch today's game against the Indians."

On the assumption that any physical torture would be preferable to another fiscal setback, Courtney said, "I'll catch!"

That afternoon Courtney collected three singles off Early Wynn, the Indians' future Hall of Famer, and earned the undying admiration of his teammates. Considering his reputation as a battler, it was ironic that in 1975 Clint Courtney should die after suffering a heart attack while playing, of all things, ping pong.

• • •

Who was the youngest high school pitcher ever to go straight from the classroom to a major league mound? In 1944, at the age of 15, Joe Nuxhall was signed by the Cincinnati Reds and was actually sent in to pitch against National League opposition. Granted, it was during World War II, when a number of stars were serving in the Armed Forces but Nuxhall, nevertheless, was a very young teenager. He pitched one inning, gave up five runs and was sent to the showers — for eight years. He returned to the Reds in 1952 and became a keystone of Cincinnati's mound corps. Others have taken a bee-line directly from the classroom to the mound, and remained in the bigs. The most notable such prodigy was Bob "Rapid Robert" Feller, who was only 17 when he turned pro with Cleveland in 1936. Feller pitched 62 innings, won five and lost three, struck out 76 and walked 47 while giving up 23 earned runs. Feller's accomplishment was astonishing when one considers that he never played a day in the minors and had only two losing seasons. Another such whiz-kid was Johnny Antonelli, who came directly from school to the Boston Braves in 1948 at the age of 18. More recently, Mike Morgan, 18, graduated high school on a Monday and signed the following Sunday with Charlie Finley's Oakland A's in 1978. He promptly started against Baltimore and allowed ten hits and two unearned runs in a 3-0 loss.

• • •

Who is the big-league general manager who, as a Giants' scout, told a teenaged Pete Rose he was too small to ever play in the majors?
The biggest bonehead decision ever made by Montreal Expos' general manager Charlie Fox occurred when he was scouting in Cincinnati for the Giants. At the time, Pete Rose was a high school baseball star with dreams of making it in the bigs. Fox took one look at Rose and shook his head, no! "I told him he was too small," Fox recalled, "and he didn't have enough to make it. Of course, he only weighed about 140 pounds and looked like a midget. He had no power. I know what he has done since, but when I saw him he lacked too much. In fact I told him 'I can't put you in a Giants' uniform, you'd look like a giant midget.' "
Rose not only emerged as a Reds' giant; on the night of July 25, 1978 Pete broke Tommy Holmes' National League record when he hit safely in his 38th consecutive game. Ironically, Rose was born April 14, 1941, the very same year that Joe DiMaggio, "The Yankee Clipper," batted safely in 56 straight games. Ahh, if Charlie Fox knew then what he knows now!

• • •

Who was a "Triple Crown" winner in both baseball and fishing?
As a member of the Boston Red Sox in 1949, Ted Williams won the "Triple Crown," hitting 39 home runs, an average of .343 and 159 runs batted in. In 1978, at age 60, Williams the sport fisherman had caught 1,000 tarpon on a flyrod; 1,000 bonefish on flies and 1,000 Atlantic salmon. No other flycaster in the world can make that statement.

110

And, surely, no other flycaster ever hit .406 in the big-leagues, as Williams did for the Red Sox in 1941!

• • •

Who was the National League catcher who threw a "beanball," thereby precipitating one of baseball's bloodiest riots?

A native of the Dominican Republic, Juan Marichal ranked among the best pitchers in the majors when he hurled for the San Francisco Giants against the Los Angeles Dodgers in 1965 when the two were arch-rivals in a battle for the pennant. In the fourth game of their series, Marichal tossed a viciously hard fastball at the head of Los Angeles' ace Maury Wills. Fortunately, Wills ducked in time but the Dodgers vowed revenge against Marichal. But, instead of one of the Los Angeles pitchers aiming for Marichal's cranium, it was catcher John Roseboro. On the first pitch after Marichal came to the plate, Juan let it sail wide. Roseboro caught the ball and made like he was returning the horsehide to the mound. However, it met an obstacle enroute — Marichal's ear — and the brawl was on. Armed with his bat, Marichal made for Roseboro's ear, and head. He achieved both targets, at least three times and won a nine-day suspension and $1,750 fine for his efforts. As for Roseboro, his "beanball" was considerably less expensive, apart from the black-and-blue marks he suffered at the expense of Marichal's Louisville Slugger.

• • •

Hank Greenberg said that the pitcher who emerged most upset from a loss was Wes Ferrell. What did Ferrell do?

Greenberg liked to recall one game in particular as typical of Ferrell's reactions to a loss. In this game Ferrell, then with the Washington Senators, found himself with a 7-0 lead in early innings. Rain began to fall and Ferrell's opponent, the Detroit Tigers, tried to slow down the game, in an effort to get it called off. But the Senators' lead seemed insurmountable, and Ferrell began to yell from his dugout that the Tigers were stalling. The game continued.

In the middle of the game Ferrell ran into difficulties and Detroit chipped at his lead until they tied in the eighth at 9-9. Ferrell was yanked.

Wes sat in the dugout, enduring the Tigers' taunts, and slowly began to tear and pick his glove apart, finally ripping out the stuffing. Next he stalked off to the locker room, where he shredded his uniform, starting with the socks. Greenberg claimed that the climax of the apparel destruction was when Ferrell picked up his watch, threw it down on the locker room floor and jumped up and down on it.

There are those who claim that a former teammate of Greenberg's — a Tiger pitcher named Fred Hutchinson — had a far worse temper than Wes Ferrell. After a painful drubbing, Hutchinson would head down the long clubhouse corridor, smashing light bulbs until the tunnel was pitch black. After the game, as Tiger players groped through the dark tunnel, they would say, "Wonder what's left of the clubhouse?"

Sure enough, not much.

• • •

Which Montreal Expos regular hit a home run in his first major-league at-bat?
Tim Wallach became the 47th player in major league history to accomplish this feat when he belted a four-baser off San Francisco Giants pitcher Phil Nastu on September 6, 1980.

• • •

While Canada is represented in the majors by Toronto and Montreal, there are Canadian clubs in Triple A

leagues sprinkled across the country. Can you name any of them?
Vancouver and Edmonton have teams in the Triple A Pacific Coast League. The Vancouver Canadians are affiliated with the Milwaukee Brewers while the Edmonton Trappers are a farm club for the California Angels.

● ● ●

Name the Canadian-born pitcher who appeared in three World Series games for the Boston Red Sox in 1975.
Reggie Cleveland of Swift Current, Saskatchewan, was the Red Sox' starting pitcher in the pivotal fifth game of the series. The teams were tied at two games apiece when Cleveland took the mound for Boston on October 16, 1975. He was yanked after the fifth inning and was tagged with the loss and Cincinnati won the game, 6-2. It gave the Reds a three games to two lead in the series. Cleveland, who was a reliever in Game Three, also made a brief appearance in the seventh and final game, also won by Boston, 4-3. Cleveland also played for the St. Louis Cardinals (1969-1973) and the Milwaukee Brewers but, unfortunately, never for the Indians. If he had, public address announcers around the American League would have had the pleasure of intoning: "Now pitching for Cleveland — CLEVELAND!"

● ● ●

Which original Toronto Blue Jays pitcher was a 20-game winner in both major leagues and also tossed a no-hitter for the Los Angeles Dodgers?
It was none other than Bill (The Singer Throwing Machine) Singer, whose no-hitter stopped the Philadelphia Phillies on July 20, 1970. Singer won 20 games for the Dodgers in 1969 and 20 for California in 1973. He joined the Blue Jays in 1977 but because of a bad shoulder was unable to regain the form that gave him his marvelous nickname.

The Singer Throwing Machine actually took several years to reach high gear. He broke in with the Dodgers in 1964 but didn't win his first game until 1967. His best season was 1969, when he won 20, lost 12 and compiled a 2.34 ERA.

• • •

The man responsible for bringing minor professional baseball to Toronto was the same executive who built the New York Yankees dynasty in the Bronx. Name this titan of the diamond game.

Edgar Grant Barrow participated in almost every facet of baseball from the managing to the executive level. Once, Nashville police escorted Barrow — then managing the Detroit Tigers — to jail for throwing a bucket of water over jeering fans during an exhibition game.

Barrow eventually became president of the International League and was instrumental in steering a franchise to Toronto. In time the Maple Leafs and the Montreal Royals became two of the most formidable minor league franchises and this success ultimately led to the two cities being awarded major league franchises.

After leaving his position with the International League, Barrow gained even greater fame as general manager of the New York Yankees (1920-1944), and the man responsible for converting George Herman (Babe) Ruth from a pitcher to an outfielder. Barrow also is the man responsible for signing the immortal Honus Wagner to his first contract.

• • •

What were the ageless Satchel Paige's six rules on staying young?

Leroy "Satchel" Paige, acclaimed as the fastest pitcher of his day, had six rules he claimed enabled him to be a pitching star as a 42-year-old rookie on the 1948 pennant-winning Cleveland Indians, after many years in the old Negro League.

They were:

1. Avoid fried meats, which angry up the blood.
2. If your stomach disputes you, lie down and pacify it with cool thoughts.
3. Keep the juices flowing by jangling around gently as you move.
4. Go very light on the vices, such as carrying on in society. The social ramble ain't restful.
5. Avoid running at all times.
6. Don't look back. Something might be gaining on you.

• • •

Can you recall when a batter hit a ball — and then ran to third?

In 1902 Jimmy St. Vrain, an unremarkable Chicago Cub pitcher, decided to hit left-handed instead of right-handed. Sure enough, he ripped a liner, and St. Vrain, delighted, took off — for *third*, completely forgetting that he was batting lefty.

As he charged third, shortstop Honus Wagner fielded the ball, looked to first — then to third, and later said, "I threw to first, but I'm not sure if that was the right play anyway!"

Fortunately for Wagner, but not for St. Vrain, it was the right play.

• • •

Who holds the Montreal Expos' record for most stolen bases in one season?

Ron LeFlore played only one season (1980) in Montreal, but it was a memorable one. The Detroit native came up with 97 stolen bases, an Expos' record. LeFlore broke in with the Detroit Tigers in 1974. After his stint in Montreal, LeFlore was signed by the Chicago White Sox.

• • •

7

1. Who did the Blue Jays play in their first game?
2. The winning pitcher that day went on to win a Cy Young Award. Can you name the pitcher?
3. What Canadian player had the nickname "Twinkle-toes?"
4. A Canadian pitcher had his career shortened by the Second World War in an unusual way. Can you recall the pitcher?
5. A current Blue Jay started and lost the first game of the 1976 World Series. Can you name him?
6. Who was the first Canadian-born manager in the bigs?
7. The second Canadian-born manager was the only one to manage both Boston teams — the Braves and the Red Sox. Who was he?
8. The king of pinch-hits was one of the original Expos! Can you name him?
9. Can you name the Canadians who led the Astros in hitting in the 1980 playoffs?
10. Only two original Expos were active in 1983. Who were they?

Answers begin on page 172.

No less than two members of the Montreal Expos have won the National League's Rookie of the Year Award. Can you name either or both of them?
Carl Morton turned the trick with an 18-11 record in 1970 and Andre Dawson did it in 1977. A righthander, Morton remained with the Expos until 1973, when he moved on to the Atlanta Braves.

As for Dawson, his Canadian roots ran deeper than simply the Expos. Andre broke into the pro ranks with Lethbridge of the Pioneer League in 1975 and moved on to Quebec City a year later. He completed his minor-league stewardship in 1976 with Denver and then moved up to Montreal, where he has starred for the Expos.

• • •

Which team won a playoff on a wild pitch?
After a tough five-game playoff, the Cincinnati Reds scored on a wild pitch to beat the Pittsburgh Pirates and win the 1972 National League Pennant.

With Pittsburgh leading, 3-2, in the bottom of the ninth inning, Johnny Bench crashed a home run off Dave Giusti to tie the score. The next batter, Tony Perez, lined a single and Denis Menke followed that with another base hit. Bob Moose came in to relieve Giusti and got Cesar Geronimo to pop a fly at Roberto Clemente. George Foster, pinch running for Perez, took third on the fly.

The next batter, Darrel Chaney, popped up to Gene Alley for the second out. But with Hal McRae batting, Moose unleashed a wild pitch to score Foster with the winning run, and give the Reds their second National League pennant in three years.

• • •

A French-Canadian pitcher from Montreal had high hopes for a long career with the Brooklyn Dodgers during the mid-1940s but he lasted only three games. Name the righthander.

Jean Pierre Roy was up for a cup of coffee. Of the three big league games in which he appeared in 1946, Roy started one and relieved in the others. Alas, he pitched a total of only 6.1 innings, gave up 5 hits, five walks and struck out six. His earned run average was a whopping 9.95. That helps explain why he was on the next train back to Montreal.

• • •

This pitcher was born in Fredericton, New Brunswick, and died in Plaster Rock, New Brunswick. He played for the St. Louis Cardinals. What is his name?
Vincent William Shields played two games for the Cardinals during the 1924 season and produced a 1-1 record, and a 3.00 earned run average. You would think that was good enough to keep him around for a while but Shields was dispatched to the minors and never saw the big leagues again.

• • •

The only native of Levis, Quebec, ever to pitch in both the National and American Leagues did so for which teams?
Both San Francisco and Minnesota provided a home for Georges Henri Maranda of Levis. Maranda appeared in the Bay Area in 1960, winning one and losing four for the Giants. He reappeared two years later, this time producing a 1-3 record in Minnesota. The 6-2, 195 pound righty then bid *adieu* to the bigs.

• • •

The 1957 Cincinnati fans voted seven members of the Reds' starting team to the All-Star opening lineup. Commissioner Ford Frick ruled that only five Reds would be allowed to start the game. Who were the five starting Reds, the two who didn't start and the three non-Reds who did?

One week prior to the 1957 All-Star Game, the Cincinnati Red fans stuffed the ballot boxes with 500,000 votes in order to see their beloved team start the game.

Ford Frick allowed Johnny Temple to start at second, with Don Hoak at third, Frank Robinson in left field, Roy McMillan at short and Ed Bailey as the catcher.

Red fans also voted Wally Post and Gus Bell to the starting lineup, but Frick replaced them with Hank Aaron and Willie Mays. Stan Musial played first base, as first baseman George Crowe was the only Reds' starter the Cincinnati fans had failed to elect.

The National League lost the game, 6-5, but the NL hitting star was Gus Bell, who had a pinch-hit double that drove in two runs.

Musial, Aaron and Mays combined for four hits in 11 at-bats, while the Cincinnati quintet went two for 11.

• • •

The New York Yankees went through six managers in four years! Can you name the participants in the merry-go-round?
George Steinbrenner, a man chronically dissatisfied with his managers, started making wholesale changes in 1980 when he replaced Billy Martin, on his second tour as manager, with Dick Howser.

Howser was a good choice; he motivated his players (including moody Reggie Jackson) and won the division title. Jackson enjoyed his best season ever, 41 homers and a .300 average. Jackson's homers tied for the league lead with Ben Oglivie.

But Howser's Yankees collapsed in the playoffs, losing in three games straight to the Kansas City Royals. Infuriated, Steinbrenner replaced Howser with Gene Michael, the team's general manager.

Michael's cautious managing and deference to George Steinbrenner kept him in first place and in charge when the strike hit in 1981. After the strike, the Yankees were declared the "first-half" winners, assured of a playoff berth. But his over-cautious managing in the second half lost games and alienated him from the players. Steinbrenner decided to change managers, bringing in Bob Lemon, who had managed the Yankees' great World Championship team in 1978.

Lemon stabilized the team, and guided it to a victory in the playoffs. But in the World Series, after the Yanks won the first two games, the Dodgers came back to win four in a row. Pitcher George Frazier lost three games for the Yanks in the series, setting a new World Series record.

Even so, Steinbrenner promised Lemon that he could manage the Yankees all the way through the '82 season, and Lemon returned to open it. But the Yankees fell apart quickly without Reggie Jackson, who had fled to the Angels after a disastrous 1981 season.

Bereft of effective power and pitching, the Yankees stumbled around until mid-May when Steinbrenner had seen enough. Out went Lemon; back came Gene Michael.

However, Michael was no improvement. One night, the Yankees lost both ends of a doubleheader to the lowly Cleveland Indians, with Steinbrenner in attendance. The fans directed their wrath at Steinbrenner, and the boss was annoyed. His first move was to allow fans to use their tickets as rainchecks for other games.

His second move was to fire Gene Michael, and bring in superscout and former pitching coach Clyde King as manager. King restored some order, but the season was too far gone to save.

When all was over, Steinbrenner changed managers again, bringing in his sixth manager, on his third trip . . . Billy Martin, the man he'd started with at the end of 1979.

Round and round goes the merry-go-round.

•　•　•

Who was the first owner to use a midget in a game?
Although Bill Veeck gets credit for putting 43-inch Eddie

Gaedel into a regular season game in 1951, it was actually Red Sox owner Tom Yawkey who put the first midget into a game.

In a 1938 exhibition game, Sox manager Joe Cronin brought 42-inch Donald Davidson in to pinch hit. Like Gaedel, Davidson walked on four pitches, and got his name into the box score.

After the Yankees clinched the pennant that season, Cronin tried it again. Pinch-hitting for catcher Moe Berg, Davidson strode to the plate carrying his fungo bat. But umpire Bill Summers sent Davidson back to the dugout, and lectured Cronin about the integrity of the game.

• • •

Name the pitcher who once went AWOL and bought a plane ticket to Israel, saying he wanted to go to Bethlehem to get "nearer to God."

Although he had a fine career with both the Red Sox and the Boston Braves, Gene Conley may be remembered best for a strange sequence of events in 1962.

Conley was going through a bad stretch with the Red Sox, and like any other pitcher on a bad ball club, was losing ball games due to non-support. He had gone 23 innings without his teammates scoring a run for him.

He was on the mound pitching against the Yankees in July when the Yankees erupted for eight runs in the third inning to chase Conley.

On the bus back to the airport, Conley had time to think about the season. After a while he decided he and teammate E.J. "Pumpsie" Green would go carousing while his teammates travelled back to Boston.

After a few drinks (Conley had scotch, Green had milk) Conley tried to convince Green to go to Israel with him.

"I had started reading the Bible about that time. The more I got tanked, the more an idea made sense to me. 'Hey,' I thought, 'I'm going to Bethlehem and Jerusalem and get all my problems straightened out and come back with a big winner.' "

Well, Green didn't go with Conley, but Conley tried to go anyway. He bought his ticket, but was refused passage because he didn't have a passport. He went to Providence *en route* to Massachusetts and resurfaced two days later.

Maybe Conley's idea was a bit crazy, but he went on to have his best year, winning 15 games.

• • •

What is the record for fewest fans at a World Series game?

Only 6,210 people showed up for the fifth and deciding game of the 1908 World Series in Detroit as the Chicago Cubs defeated the Tigers, 2-0. Orvie Overall outpitched Wild Bill Donovan.

Another record was set at that time; the game took one hour and 25 minutes to play, the shortest time in World Series annals.

• • •

Name the American League team that had five players hit 25 or more homers in one season.

One of the greatest home-run-hitting teams ever, the 1977 Boston Red Sox had five players hit at least 25 homers. Jim Rice, in his third full season with the Red Sox, hit 39 home runs, leading the American League. George Scott, who was traded back to the Sox on December 6, 1976, hit 33. Butch Hobson, playing his first season with Boston, sacked 30 round-trippers. Captain Carl Yastrzemski hit 28, while Carlton Fisk matched a career high 26 homers.

The Red Sox hit 213 that year, making them one of the most powerful lineups in baseball. But they lost the pennant as the pitching fell short in cozy Fenway Park.

• • •

Name the pitcher who holds the record for most saves in World Series history.

After playing in three consecutive World Series, Rollie Fingers compiled six saves for the Oakland A's, a Series record. Fingers had two saves against Cincinnati in the 1972 World Series. He saved one game the next year against the Mets, then saved three games against the LA Dodgers in the 1974 World Series.

• • •

Phillie pitching star Kirby Higbe, Jr. was once nearly arrested in New York. Can you recall the encounter with New York's finest?

Kirby Higbe once lost the opener of a doubleheader in the Polo Grounds, 1-0, in eleven innings. In the second game, he was called in to hold the fort in the final inning with the score tied.

Higby recalled, "So I go in. The first batter hits an easy grounder to Del Young at short, and Del nearly takes Mayor La Guardia's head off in the box seats with his throw. The runner goes to second, so I walk the batter. A bunt then pushes them over, so I walk the next batter to pitch to Ott. Ott hits an easy, shallow fly to center. The runner isn't even tagging, but Joe Marty catches the ball and unleashes a throw to the screen. I lost both games that day.

"After the game, Doc Prothro tells us to go out and get drunk. Hell, he didn't have to tell us. A group of us went up to my room at the hotel and broke into a couple of bottles. Pretty soon Del had too much to drink and tosses an empty bottle right through the hotel window.

"It wasn't long before a cop was knocking at the door. I answered. 'Yes, officer, what can I do for you?'

" 'You're Kirby Higbe, aren't you?' he says.

" 'That's right, officer.'

" 'Who in hell threw that bottle out the window? Nearly went through the roof of a taxi.'

" 'Just a bunch of us Phillies, having a little too much to drink.'

"The cop just laughed. As he turned to leave, he smiled and said, 'Hell, I don't blame you. If I were with the Phillies I'd have thrown *myself* out the window.' "

• • •

Name the only team to drop a triple header.
Due to a scheduling problem, the Brooklyn Dodgers had to play three games against the Pittsburgh Pirates on June 2, 1903. Pittsburgh was on its way to become the first National League team to appear in the World Series, while Brooklyn was finishing up a fifth-place season.

The Pirates came into Brooklyn and swept all three games from the Dodgers, making it the only time a team ever lost a triple header.

• • •

Name the World-Series-winning team with the lowest batting average.
If their team ERA hadn't been 2.13 for the 1906 season, it's doubtful that the Chicago White Sox would have beaten the Yankees to win the pennant. The White Sox batted just .228 in the regular season, and only .198 in the World Series. But the "hitless wonders" won the AL Pennant and then defeated the powerful Chicago Cubs four game to two to win their first World Series.

• • •

Which team scored 14 runs in one inning?
During their heartbreaking season in 1948, the Boston Red Sox nailed the Philadelphia Athletic pitchers for 14 runs in the seventh inning on the Fourth of July. During a wild seventh inning, nineteen men came up to bat. The Red Sox won the game 20-8, but later lost a one-game playoff to the Indians, losing the 1948 pennant.

• • •

Name the Canadian entrepreneur who once owned the Toronto Maple Leafs baseball club, but ultimately became better known for his investments in hockey and football.

Jack Kent Cooke, one of the most flamboyant sports promoters of the past three decades, owned a good chunk of the Toronto Maple Leafs baseball team in the International League, until it became apparent that the Leafs were losing their grasp on the public. Besides, the Leafs were minor league and Cooke was never satisfied with anything less than the top drawer.

Cooke had hoped to persuade the Toronto city fathers to build a new stadium for his team so that he could move it into the majors, but when this hope was dashed in the 1960s he turned to other sports. Eventually he moved on to buy a quarter share of the Washington Redskins football team, and he paid $5,175,000 for the Los Angeles Lakers of the National Basketball Association.

A hockey nut more than anything, Cooke made his bid for a National Hockey League franchise in February 1966 and got an okay from the governors. It was Cooke who financed "The Fabulous Forum" at Inglewood, California, home of the Los Angeles Kings and the Lakers. "It's the most beautiful arena in the world," said Cooke. And while some might doubt the claim, few could argue with Cooke's success in sports, underlined years later when his Washington Redskins won the Super Bowl.

•   •   •

When and where did the first baseball All-Star Game take place outside the United States?

It was appropriate that the Montreal Expos, Canada's first major league baseball team, host the first non-American All-Star Game. In that 1982 contest at Montreal, the National League defeated the American League, 4-1.

•   •   •

John McGraw once chewed out an outfielder for making a perfect throw to the plate. Who made the perfect throw and why was McGraw irate?

Al Moore, an outfielder with a strong arm, was once sent in by McGraw in the late innings. With a runner on second, the batter singled to left. Moore threw all the way to the plate on the fly, nailing the runner and ending the inning.

Giants' fans cheered lustily, but McGraw was unimpressed. Instead, he said to Moore, "I thought I explained to you that I always wanted throws from the outfield to take one hop, in case a cutoff was necessary. You probably think you've made a fine throw. You've heard those fans cheering you and you think you're big stuff. I'll show you how big you are in relation to the team.

"Suppose I put up a sign which says, 'Tomorrow afternoon there will be a throwing exhibition by Al Moore at the Polo Grounds.' How many fans do you think it would attract? You wouldn't get fifty. I could and should fine you fifty, but I won't. In the future, just remember that the fans came here to see the Giants play, not to see Al Moore exercise his arm."

Moore repeated this story later on — for the benefit of a young man named Joe DiMaggio.

• • •

By the end of the 1983 baseball season only two of the original Blue Jays were still on the roster of the Toronto Club. Who were they?

Catcher Ernie Whitt became a Blue Jay after one season (1976) with the Boston Red Sox. The Blue Jays were the first major league team to sign Jim Clancy (1977). After seven years with the American League club he had compiled a 66-81 won-lost record and a 4.35 earned run average.

• • •

What star player went through four consecutive seasons without hitting a home run?

Although he hit 37 home runs in his career, Roger "Doc" Cramer of the Boston Red Sox went from 1936 to 1939 without hitting a single home run.

As a Philadelphia Athletic, Cramer hit 22 home runs in seven seasons. After being traded to the Boston Red Sox, Cramer hit only one home run in five seasons at Fenway Park.

Although he led the league in at-bats seven times, Cramer never had more than eight home runs in one year. He retired with a .296 batting average over 20 years.

• • •

Who holds the record for lowest ERA (minimum of 25 innings) in his World Series career?

In 25 1/3 innings, Jack Billingham of the Cincinnati Reds gave up just one earned run.

Billingham pitched in three World Series with the Reds (1972, 1975, 1976) and appeared in seven games. He combined with Clay Carroll to pitch a shutout in 1972, and wound up his career with a remarkable 0.36 ERA in World Series competition.

• • •

Who led the National League in strikeouts seven years in a row, something no other pitcher has ever done?

It hardly seems likely that a pitcher who didn't win his first game in the major leagues until he was 31 years old would earn such an auspicious record. But Dazzy Vance fought against all odds to break records and win himself a place in the Hall of Fame.

Vance had problems with his right arm from the inception of his career. He was never really sure what was wrong with it, either. Dazzy was sent to the minors for the 1916 season. For the next five years, his pitching record suffered because of that sore arm. Sometimes his arm hurt so badly that he didn't want to pitch and he hardly could. He had no alternatives to playing baseball; it was the only thing he knew how to do, and he had to support his family somehow.

For a time, he soaked his arm in ice water. After a while, though, even that remedy didn't work. A doctor told Vance that if he laid off pitching for four or five years, it would probably stop bothering him. Dazzy's response to the doctor was "and how am I going to eat in the meantime?"

Vance was supposed to play for the Toledo, Ohio, team in the 1917 season. During spring training, he looked terrific. As soon as the season started, he tired easily and was soon being whipped by the opposition. Vance moved to Memphis, but the same fate awaited him there. At first, he'd shut out the batters with his fast ball, and then he'd get worn out and have to leave the game. He pitched two games for the Yanks in 1918 and then returned to the minors. Spencer Abbott, manager of the Memphis team, traded Vance to New Orleans. He had no time or patience for someone who couldn't perform.

After about two weeks with New Orleans, Vance's arm began to feel better, and his pitching picked up. The following season with New Orleans, he won 21 games. By chance, his performance attracted the attention of the Brooklyn Dodgers.

Hank DeBerry was a New Orleans catcher who was being noticed by the major leagues. Larry Sutton, the Dodgers' top scout, was sent out to look at DeBerry, since the Dodgers needed a catcher badly. Sutton returned to Wilbert Robinson, manager of the Brooklyn team, to report that they should take both DeBerry and Vance.

Vance was now 31 years old, had played with a dozen different teams, and was well known for his sore arm. Nevertheless, Dazzy became a Dodger. One night in a spring exhibition game against the St. Louis Browns, Vance was pitching and faced George Sisler, one of the greatest hitters of all time. Vance threw the first pitch and it was a strike. The second pitch was a strike, too. With the two strikes on Sisler, Vance wound up and sent a curve ball flying toward the plate. Sisler knew he was out.

Robinson was ecstatic. He hadn't known what a good buy he had found. "Anyone who can catch Sisler looking at a curve must be throwing a pretty good one," commented the Dodger manager.

From that point on, Vance was a first-rate player. In his first full season, he won 18 games and led the league in strike-outs. His second season was a duplicate of the first. His third season was better — 28 wins and only six losses. He was voted MVP.

No other pitcher has done what Vance did — he led the league in strikeouts for seven years in a row! Upon his retirement, Dazzy had won 197 games and struck out 2,045 batters. Vance was forty-five before he gave up the game. In 1954, he was voted into the Hall of Fame.

• • •

Who did Ted Williams strike out in his only pitching appearance in the major leagues?

Rudy York. Williams, who began his baseball career as a pitcher-outfielder in the Pacific Coast League, pestered Joe Cronin, the Red Sox manager, to let him pitch a game. When the Sox were out of the pennant race, Cronin let Williams pitch the last two innings of a game on August 24, 1940. Jim Bagby, the Boston pitcher, and Williams switched positions, with Bagby going to the outfield. Williams allowed three hits and one run, and had one strikeout (York). Detroit won the game, 12-1.

• • •

Can you recall how teams travelled before coast-to-coast jets were the norm?

Trains, which created a camaraderie that wouldn't exist later on.

One night in New York's Grand Central Terminal, the

Brooklyn Dodgers were boarding their train, when a rookie who had gone four-for-four as a regular found himself assigned to an upper berth. He angrily sought out travelling secretary Harold Parrott.

"How come I'm assigned to an upper berth?" the rookie demanded. "I went four-for-four as a regular. I thought regulars get to sleep in a lower berth."

Parrott hustled off in search of manager Leo Durocher. Moments later, he came back with a solution. "Durocher says you are to sleep in the upper. He says you're not a regular anymore!"

Yogi Berra enjoyed train travel, insisting that his career would have lasted longer if he had been able to ride the train more often. "It was a fun way to travel and a lot of us would look forward to a road trip. We'd arrive, let's say in Chicago, and feel refreshed."

Burleigh Grimes, however, who pitched 25 years before Berra caught, complained about train cars being hot, and repeatedly getting covered with soot when trying to open a window.

Pitcher Jesse Haines remembered "playing a double-header in St. Louis in August, hot as blazes. When it was over we had to rush like the devil to catch a train for Boston. You couldn't open the window or else you'd get covered with cinders. So you just lay there and sweated. When we got to Boston, we had to play a game right away."

• • •

Which batter was the most difficult to strike out?
In a career that spanned 14 seasons, Joe Sewell became the toughest man to strike out in Major League history. Sewell, who played for the Indians and Yankees, struck out once every 62.6 times at bat.

Sewell had a career batting average of .312, and was elected to the Hall of Fame in 1977.

• • • •

Which American League team hit five home runs in one inning?

The fireworks occurred on June 9, 1966 when five members of the Minnesota Twins blasted homers in the seventh inning.

The Twins, who won the AL pennant the previous season, pulled home runs out of Rich Rollins, Zoilo Versalles, Tony Oliva, Don Mincher and Harmon Killebrew to break the previous American League record of four homers in one inning.

• • •

Name the last player to hit three home runs in one game in both leagues.

In a feat only duplicated by Babe Ruth and Johnny Mize, Claudell Washington hit three home runs in one game in both leagues.

Washington had his first three-home run game as a member of the Chicago White Sox on July 14, 1979. He was traded to the New York Mets in 1980, and on June 22 of that same year, he hit three home runs in one game against the Los Angeles Dodgers, in Chavez Ravine.

• • •

It is a well-known fact that Babe Ruth was dubbed "The Sultan of Swat." Do you know who "The Rabbi of Swat" was?

Back in 1923 Giants' scout Dick Kinsella brought up a boy named Moses Solomon to manager John McGraw. McGraw worried about the fame that Babe Ruth was bringing to the rival Yanks. He was afraid that one day the Giants would play second fiddle to the Yanks. Someone had to be found to attract fans to the Giants as well. McGraw knew it would be impossible to find another Ruth. The only thing he could hope for was to keep bringing in new and impressive names to the Giants. McGraw knew that Bill Terry, Frankie Frisch, Dave Bancroft and

Lindy Lindstrom would certainly draw, but enough to counteract the Babe?

Then McGraw came up with a new idea. Observing how many Jewish people in Upper Manhattan and the Bronx were loyal baseball fans, he reasoned that bringing a good Jewish player to the team might attract attention, and woo the Jewish fans from Babe and the Yanks. That's when Kinsella found Moses Solomon.

Proclaiming that "Solomon is as big as a house, can play first base like Sisler, hit like Ruth, and fight like Dempsey," Kinsella told reporters that his new friend was "the million-dollar player McGraw has been seeking." All these extravagant claims left the other Giants a little skeptical about Solomon. Nonetheless, they quickly found him a suitable nickname — "The Rabbi of Swat."

Solomon's career was, unfortunately, short-lived. He appeared in only two games. Making three hits in those two trials, it looked as though he would live up to his new nickname. McGraw realized, however, that Solomon was just too crude for major league competition. By the end of the year, Solomon had played for Toledo, Pittsfield, Waterbury and Bridgeport. He then disappeared from the game.

The Dodgers had the identical problem; they had to find players to compete with Ruth's fame as well. Dodger owner Charles Ebbets came up with what he thought was the answer. Wally Simpson, who "hit almost as many home runs as Solomon," was Ebbets' answer to the problem. "He's a Yonkers boy with a big local following, and you're going to be hearing plenty about him," declared the Dodgers' chieftain.

But Brooklyn heard less about Simpson than they did about Solomon. Simpson suffered an injury on ice that winter, reporting to the Dodgers with a sprained ankle. In one game against the Phillies, he stepped in as a pinch hitter, chalked up a double and then retired from the game after his sister's funeral.

Neither Simpson nor Solomon, both seemingly promising players, were the answers to Ruth's fame.

• • •

In 1934 which famous manager insulted the Dodgers by asking, "Is Brooklyn still in the League?"

Never before had Dodger fans been so outraged. In 1934 at a pre-season press conference, New York Giants manager Bill Terry responded to a reporter's question, "How about Brooklyn?" with an insult that Dodger fans would not withstand. "Is Brooklyn still in the league?" quipped the manager.

The New York Giants had won the National League pennant and the World Series. Bill Terry was a successful manager determined to lead the Giants to victory throughout the 1934 season.

From the moment he uttered those words, Dodger fans vowed revenge. Toward the end of the season, the Giants and the Cardinals were tied. Both teams went home to play their final two games. The Reds met the Cards in St. Louis, while the Giants and the Dodgers battled it out in New York. At last the sixth-place Dodgers had their chance to pounce on the Giants in an act of pure revenge.

The first game was almost rained out, but instead started 40 minutes late. In the fifth inning, Dodger pitcher Van Lingle Mungo singled, advanced to second on a walk, and scored on Lonnie Frey's single. The Dodgers scored again in the sixth and seventh, earning them a 3-0 lead.

In the seventh, George Watkins homered for the first Giant run. But the Dodgers wrapped up the game in the ninth with two single runs off Al Smith for a 5-1 victory.

The Cards destroyed the Reds in St. Louis as Daffy Dean pitched a six-hitter, ending the game 6-1. The Cardinals pulled ahead of the Giants.

Dodger fans were ready for action at the second game and final day of the season. No longer the front runner, the

Giants ripped through the first inning with four runs. The Dodgers picked up a run in the second and fourth innings, a homer by Freddie Fitzsimmons gave the Giants five runs, while Brooklyn scored again in the fifth inning, bringing it to 5-3.

Hal Schumacher came in to pitch for the Giants. Suddenly, a roar rose from the stadium as the scoreboard indicated the Cards were ahead of the Reds 5-0 in the fourth. Moments later, a Dodger run off a wild pitch tied the score in their game.

An actionless ninth inning brought the two teams head to head in the tenth. Brooklyn, still vividly remembering Bill Terry's comment, sent their batters hitting again. Sam Leslie singled and advanced to third on a double by Tony Cuccinello. Giant pitcher Schumacher was out and Carl Hubbell came in. After Johnny Babich's out, Hubbell intentionally walked Joe Stripp, loading the bases. Al Lopez bounced into what was supposed to be a double play to short, but King Carl's strategy backfired. Blondy Ryan fumbled and Johnny McCarthy, in for Leslie, scored. Two more runs scored as Brooklyn finished the Giants off, 8-5.

Important though it was that the Cards blanked Cincinnati 9-0, Dodger fans were more relieved that they had avenged Terry's insult. His comment had indirectly kicked the highly unpopular Giants right out of the pennant.

● ● ●

Can you recall the two Hall of Fame inductees for 1983? You're right if you selected Juan Antonio Marichal and Brooks Calbert Robinson.

A native of Laguna Verde, Montecristi, Dominican Republic, Marichal broke into the National League in 1960 with the San Francisco Giants and remained the righthanded pitching star of that club until 1973 when he was sold to the Boston Red Sox. His major league career ended in 1975 with the Los Angeles Dodgers.

Marichal pitched a total of 471 games, won 243 and lost 142. His lifetime earned run average was 2.89. In championship games, Marichal's record was modest. In the one championship series game he pitched, Marichal was tagged with the loss in 1971. He also pitched four innings of a 1962 World Series game, gave up two hits but did not figure in the decision.

Among his claims to fame, Marichal can cite the following: he established the National League record for most season opening games won (six), 1962, 1964, 1966 and 1971 through 1973. He pitched a 1-0 no-hit victory against Houston on June 15, 1963. He led the National League in shutouts with ten in 1965 and eight in 1969. He led the National League in complete games with 22 in 1964 and 30 in 1968.

Robinson, a third baseman, spent his entire major league career in Baltimore, starting in 1955 and ending in 1977. A native of Little Rock, Arkansas, Robinson — like Marichal — was inducted into the Baseball Hall of fame at Cooperstown, New York on July 31, 1983.

Robinson set several major league records during his stewardship with the Orioles: most years leading league in games, third baseman (8); most double plays, third baseman, lifetime (618), most games, third baseman, lifetime (2,896); most putouts, third baseman, lifetime (2,697); most assists, third baseman, lifetime (6,205); most chances accepted, third baseman, lifetime (8,902); highest fielding average, third baseman, lifetime (.971); most seasons leading league, assists, third baseman (8); most seasons, third baseman (23); most seasons, one club (23); most consecutive seasons, one club (23); most seasons leading league, fielding, third baseman (11).

● ● ●

Stratford-on-Avon was home to William Shakespeare, but Stratford, Ontario, was home to a different kind of big-leaguer. Who was he?

Larry Landreth, a righthander for the Montreal Expos in 1976 and 1977, hailed from the Ontario home of the Shakespeare Festival. In two big league seasons Landreth produced one win and three losses. He clearly was not as accomplished a big-leaguer as the Bard of Avon.

• • •

Long before the Expos were admitted to the National League a Montreal-to-the-Majors axis existed. Which teams were involved?
The Montreal Royals of the International League was a Brooklyn Dodgers farm team for many years and many big-league stars (including Jackie Robinson and Roy Campanella) got their start in Canada. When the Dodgers were in their heyday during the late 1940s and early 1950s, the big club was loaded so heavily with talent that many fine ball players were kept on the farm team in Montreal. The Royals, in that era, were considered the equal of many big league teams.

• • •

How did the mighty Babe lose a home run?
Contrary to popular belief that the Babe hit 714 career regular-season homeruns, he actually hit 715 in his illustrious career. The only hitch was that he did not receive credit for a roundtripper he hit on July 8, 1918. According to baseball rules before 1920, when a team batting last won the game in the ninth or in an extra inning, they could not win by more than one run. If a man hit an outside-the-park home run with any base runners, which would have resulted in a victory by more than one run, he was given credit for a lesser hit and only the winning run would score.

Thirty-six others who played within the span of 1884-1920 also lost home runs because of this rule.

• • •

8

1. Cal Ripken, Jr., and Robin Yount won the American League's Most Valuable Player Award in 1983 and 1982, respectively. Who was the last shortstop to win it before them?

2. Who were the first two players to be selected by the Baseball Writers Association of America as MVP in their respective leagues?

3. Name the only six non-Yankees to win the MVP award two years in a row?

4. Name the last Yankee pitcher to throw a no-hitter before Dave Righetti did on July 4, 1983.

5. Name the four Oakland hurlers who combined efforts for a no-hitter. (Name the date, year, the opposing team and the final score for extra credit!)

6. Who won the Cy Young awards for their respective leagues in 1967?

7. In 1973, California's Nolan Ryan struck out an amazing 383 batters to lead the major leagues. Do you remember who finished second?

8. Who made the only error in the first All-Star game?

9. Who was the first manager of the Toronto Blue Jays?

10. Who is the all-time leader for third baseman in participating in or initiating double plays?

Answers begin on page 172.

Who was the only first baseman to go through an entire nine-inning contest without touching the ball?

Next to the pitcher and the catcher, the first baseman usually plays a bigger part in the scheme of things than any other player on the field. But such was not the case on September 27, 1930, in a game between the Chicago White Sox and the St. Louis Browns. Chisox' first baseman Bud Clancy had the easiest day in the history of first sacking. On that day, Clancy had not a single play to make — not a putout nor an assist nor a chance throughout the entire nine-inning contest. Must've been a lot of outfield flies!

• • •

Name the first pitcher who hurled five complete games in one World Series.

In the 1903 World Series Pittsburgh Pirate pitcher Charles Louis "Deacon" Phillippe, aided by two rainouts during the inaugural Fall Classic, pitched and completed five games versus the American League Champion Boston Red Sox.

In Game 1 Phillippe struck out ten and got credit for the win. The Pirates exploded for four runs in the first inning and went on to an easy 7-3 victory. After Boston's Bill Dinneen evened the Series at one game apiece, Phillippe returned to win Game Three, allowing only four Red Sox hits in his second nine-inning stint. The Pirates again scored early and won the game 4-2. The Pirates then took a seemingly commanding 3-1 edge as they sent Phillippe out to the mound for his third start in four games, after two days of rain had given the needed rest. He managed to halt a three-run Boston ninth inning in time to preserve a 5-4 victory.

After the Red Sox won Games Five and Six, Deacon was called on to bring the Pirates their fourth victory in the best-of-nine series. This time he faltered and yielded 11 hits — five of them triples *en route* to a 7-3 setback.

Following two cancellations by rain Game Eight was

finally played with Phillippe again on the hill for the Pirates, who were then looking to stave off elimination. The Pirate hurler lasted the whole game, but was hit hard as the Red Sox claimed the World Championship winning 3-0. Still, to Phillippe's credit, he had completed five games in one Series, the first pitcher ever to do so.

• • •

Can you recall the player who hit three home runs in one inning?
The first night game in Waco, Texas, had a large audience at the game and an even larger one following it on radio. But the game played on August 6, 1930, was to be memorable for other reasons.

At the top of the eighth inning Waco was behind, 6-2. and Jerry Mallet, the Beaumont pitcher, showed no signs of relaxing. Gene Rye was the first batter up for the Waco team. He sent a pitch sailing over the right field fence for his first home run. Mallet then allowed a walk, a single, and another walk before he was taken out of the game. The Waco team now had enough men on base to tie the score.

Mallet's relief, Ed Green, was not much better. First Waco tied the score. Then runs started pouring across the plate like mad. Green was called out of the game after allowing seven runs and not a single out. The third pitcher for that inning was Walter Newman.

Gene Rye was the first batter Newman faced. It was his second time at bat for the inning and there were two men on base. Rye cracked another line drive over the right field fence. Ten runs had scored with still no outs.

Finally, one batter was out, followed by Tony Pier's home run. Eventually, with bases loaded and two outs, Rye was at bat again. The second pitch sailed over the center fielder's head and the fence behind him. A grand slam!

By the end of the inning, the Waco team had scored 18 runs, with Gene Rye hitting three home runs and batting in eight. No other professional player since 1930 has equalled Rye's performance.

And that wasn't even the majors!

• • •

In 1927, three teams won all the offensive categories in the American League. What were they?
Harry Heilman of Detroit led the league in batting averages (.398). George Sisler of St. Louis led the league in stolen bases (27), and Yankees led in every other major category. The Yanks not only led in most of the categories, but they were second and sometimes third in most of them as well. Earle Combs led the league in at-bats (648), hits (231), and triples (23). Ruth led in home runs (60), runs (158), walks (138), and strikeouts (89). Gehrig led in doubles (52) and RBIs (175). Gehrig was also second in home runs (47) and Lazzeri third (18). Ruth was second in RBIs (164). Gehrig was second in runs (149) and Combs third (137). Gehrig was first in extra-base hits, Ruth falling in second. They traded places for slugging percentages — Ruth first (.772), and Gehrig second (.765).

• • •

Bill Dickey was chosen by the Baseball Writers' Association as the 1936 All-Star catcher. Just days later, he went on to the World Series, batting a miserable .120. Do you remember the circumstances responsible for Dickey's weak batting performance?
Despite Dickey's poor showing at the batter's box, he offered no excuses or explanations. The real story did not emerge until the following season at training camp. Through an unintentional slip-up it became known that Bill Dickey played six games of a World Series with a hand fractured in two places! A week before the end of the season, Dickey's knuckles and a pitched ball collided, causing the injury.

Removing Dickey from the team would have disrupted

the Yankees' morale. Instead, the catcher stayed in the games, taking the pounding of speed balls on a fractured hand without so much as a wince.

When asked who had thrown the damaging pitch, Dickey didn't even remember. He held no grudges.

•   •   •

Which batter left the plate after only two strikes, refusing to stay for the official end of the out?

Walter Johnson was unquestionably one of the greatest pitchers who ever lived. Yet his pitching strategy was simple and straightforward. He relied on his fast ball. If it failed to work the first time, he'd throw a faster one the next time. Batters often excuse their strike outs by explaining, "How can you hit 'em, if you can't see 'em?"

One time Ray Chapman faced the unhittable Johnson. After two swinging strikes, Chapman walked out of the batter's box and headed for the dugout in disgust.

"Wait a minute," the umpire called after him, "you've got another strike coming."

"Never mind," replied Chapman, "I don't want it."

•   •   •

When a batter strikes out in the scorebook, they represent this with the letter "K." How did the letter "K" come to stand for a strikeout?

In order to expedite things, Henry Chadwick, the father of baseball, organized the scorebook according to the last letter of the word that described the action in question. "K" was taken from the word "struck," "D" from "bound," which meant catching the ball on one hop (an out in those days), and "L" from foul.

•   •   •

What year is considered the best season ever for a pitcher, and who is credited with it?

The year was 1884 when Charles (Old Hoss) Radbourn

went 60-12, had an ERA of 1.38, pitched 678 2/3 innings, starting and finishing 72 games. He pitched underhanded, the pitcher's mound was 50 feet from the plate, it took 6 balls to constitute a walk, and 5 strikes were a strikeout. Foul tips and foul balls did not count as strikes. He also played infield on the days he didn't pitch.

• • •

The World Series of 1924 ended on a bounce!! What actually happened?

It was the twelfth inning of the seventh game between the Washington Senators and the New York Giants. Muddy Ruel was on second with Earl McNeely at bat. Earl hit one of Jack Bentley's curve balls down the third base line. New York's Fred Lindstrom readied himself in the field for the play, when the ball struck a pebble, bounced over Lindstrom's head, and sailed toward left field. Ruel rounded third and headed home for the run, which gave the Senators a world championship.

• • •

Who pitched a record nineteen straight victories for the New York Giants?

Richard William Marquard. In 1912, "Rube" Marquard started this record on opening day, April 11, with a defeat of the Dodgers. For the first half of the season, he whipped them all: Dodgers, Braves, Phillies and others. After nineteen games in succession, Rube was a wreck: "I hope it's over soon," he said. "I can't stand this much longer."

Indeed, it was over soon. Jimmy Lavender, a rookie hurler for the Cubs, broke Marquard's streak, as the Cubs won, 7-2.

Marquard wound up with a 26-11 record, a 2.57 ERA for 1912 and 201 lifetime wins.

• • •

Which player hit safely in all 14 World Series games in which he played?

While playing for Pittsburgh in the 1960 and 1971 World Series, Roberto Clemente hit safely in all the games he played. Clemente connected safely in all seven games of the 1960 World Series against the Yankees, collecting nine hits and averaging .310.

In 1971 he rapped Oriole pitching for 12 hits and two home runs to lead the Pirates. Overall, Clemente had five extra base hits in the Series, while batting .414. He wound up with a World Series average of .362 in fourteen games.

• • •

Name the player who committed four errors on *one* batted ball.

Mike Grady was playing third base for the New York Giants when a slow ground ball came his way. Little did he know that this play would put him into the record books. Grady juggled the ball, allowing the runner to reach first safely. Error one. When Mike finally got hand on horsehide, he uncorked a wild throw, which sailed over the first baseman's head by ten feet. Error two.

The runner sprinted down to second and turned toward third as the first baseman recovered Grady's errant throw, and returned it to the third baseman. The ball arrived well ahead of the sliding runner, but Mike dropped it. Error three.

As Grady scrambled to retrieve the rolling ball, the runner bolted for home. Mike had plenty of time to gun down the runner, but instead he hastily whizzed the ball five feet above the leaping catcher's mitt. Error four.

Poor Mike Grady!

• • •

What was the name of the pitcher who would scrawl the letters "N" and "G" on the baseline before the start of each game he pitched?

Alva "Bobo" Holloman, pitching for the St. Louis Browns, was the eccentric who would scrawl the initials of his wife, Nan, and son, Gary Lee, for luck.

Holloman had another claim to fame. When he made his major league debut, he pitched a no-hitter against the Philadelphia Athletics on May 6, 1953, in front of 2,500 rain-soaked fans in St. Louis.

● ● ●

Since 1901, which player has had the lowest home run total to win the home run crown?

The record belongs to Tommy Leach of the Pittsburgh Pirates. In 1902 Leach hit just six homers to win the home run title. A lifetime .269 hitter, Leach finished his career with 62 home runs. That was in the "dead-ball days," when most homers were inside-the-park affairs.

● ● ●

What batter thought it was bad luck to have his picture taken while holding his bat?

Odd though it sounds, Honus Wagner, a very superstitious man, thought that posing with his bat in his hands would be disastrous. In fact, after one photographer took an unauthorized picture of Wagner, Honus flung his bat at the camera.

● ● ●

How did an infielder discover a gold mine under a playing field?

Many infielders complain of balls that take bad bounces, disrupting an anticipated play. On occasion, however, balls have been known to take a favorable bounce, falling into a successful play. According to legend, first baseman William Griffiths had one of those lucky, unexpected bounces.

It was 1905 in Salt Lake City and Griffiths was playing first base for a team called the Rhyolites. Des Beatty, a batter for the opposition, knocked a ground ball to Griffiths. The ball struck a pebble on its way to first base and landed right in Griffith's glove. Griffiths decided the pebble was in his way sitting there on the playing field, and so he went over, picked it up, and started to throw it away. He took a second look at the pebble and noticed that it was "free" gold. He surreptitiously placed it in his pocket and continued the game.

Later, Griffiths returned to the ball park and spent an hour scratching around for more gold rocks. Eventually, he accumulated a small pailful. He informed two friends of his discovery and together they quietly bought the park.

Griffiths named the mine "First Base," and assuredly never resented the "bad" bounce that ball had taken. Because of it, Griffiths became a wealthy man.

• • •

The Philadelphia A's employed a former ballplayer as a coach in charge of an unusual job. What was it and who was he?

"Old Dan" Murphy, after ending his outfield career, became a coach for the A's, and had a simple and unique job: steal the other team's signals and relay them to the A's.

He used all kinds of strategems, usually sitting on a rooftop across the street from Shibe Park, crossing and uncrossing his legs as he observed the pitcher and catcher. One time he used a weather vane to tip off his hitters to the opposition's pitching signals, but a gale spun the vane, and only confused the A's' sluggers.

Though Murphy was the first sign-stealing coach, sign-stealing has been a major league baseball tradition. Naturally, showman Bill Veeck elevated it when he stationed a utility infielder with binoculars in his scoreboard in Cleveland to pick up signs.

And just as naturally, Veeck denied doing it.

• • •

Who were the players on Ty Cobb's All-Time Best team?
In 1945, Hall of Fame historian E.J. Lanigan wrote to Ty
Cobb asking him who would comprise his all-star team.
Cobb's answer:

Pitchers: Big Ed Walsh, Walter Johnson, Grover Cleveland Alexander, Christy Mathewson and Eddie Plank

Catchers: Mickey Cochrane and Bill Dickey

First Base: George Sisler

Second Base: Eddie Collins

Shortstop: Honus Wagner

Third Base: Buck Weaver

Left Field: Joe Jackson

Center Fielder: Tris Speaker

Right Field: Babe Ruth

Cobb wrote to Lanigan: "Note that I have placed Weaver
and Jackson, only judging them on their ability. (He was
referring to their involvement in the 1919 "Black Sox"
scandal.) I never saw Pie Traynor . . . To my way of thinking, no contest at second base: Hornsby couldn't catch a
pop fly, much less go in the outfield after them, could not
come in on a slow hit; Lajoie could not go out, nor come in,
and did not cover too much ground to his right or left. Collins could do it all, besides being a great base stealer and
base runner." (Eddie Collins got 3,000 hits, and never won
a batting title. He played in the same league as Ty Cobb.)

• • •

**Washington Senators' Manager Joe Cantillon had the
unusual nickname of "Pongo." How did he acquire this
monicker?**
When Cantillon was playing for San Francisco in the
minors at the turn of the century, baseball writer Charlie
Dryden received a written request for Joe Cantillon's
ethnic background.

Dryden, a wit, wrote with tongue firmly lodged in cheek,
"Cantillon's real name is Pelipe Pongo Cantiliono. He's an
Italian nobleman who fled to America to escape an idle life

of social ease." The Italian fans of San Francisco immediately made the Irish Cantillon their favorite. The cry of "Pongo, Pongo" reverberated throughout the stands, but whenever rooters tried to talk to Cantillon in Italian, he would snarl at them, and they would draw away.

Nevertheless, the nickname stood and it was Pongo Joe Cantillon who would manage the Senators from 1907 to 1909.

• • •

In which Canadian city did Babe Ruth hit his first home run as a professional?
Visiting Toronto on September 5, 1914 with the Providence minor league club, Ruth not only hit a home run but also pitched a one-hit shutout. Curiously, the round-tripper would be the Babe's only home run of his brief minor-league career.

• • •

Two managers did very well in the majors after their stints in the dugout and on the coaching lines for the Toronto Maple Leafs of the International League. Can you name them?
Sparky Anderson and Dick Williams have both managed World Series-winners since they graduated from the Leafs.

• • •

In 1919 and 1920 two major changes came about that would set the stage for Babe Ruth's assault on the record book. What were they?
In 1919, the new cork-centered ball was used in all games. It had previously been used only in a few games and the World Series. In 1920, all trick pitches were banned. Pitchers who had used the spitball prior to 1920 were allowed to finish their careers with it.

• • •

How long did it take Babe Ruth to break the career home run record?

Ruth passed Roger Connor's lifetime mark of 136 in his third season as a full-time player. Although Henry Aaron hit more HR's in his career and Roger Maris hit more in a season, it can be safely said that Babe Ruth was the greatest home run hitter baseball has ever seen. The facts speak for themselves. Ruth hit home run number 60 in his 151st game. Maris had 58 by his 151st game. It took Ruth 8399 at-bats to hit 714 HR's. In 8399 AB's Henry Aaron had 488 HR's. Ruth was the first player to hit 30 HR's, 40 HR's, 50 HR's and 60 HR's in a season. When he hit his 714th career HR he had more than twice as many as anybody else. Lou Gehrig, Joe DiMaggio, Ted Williams, Henry Aaron and Carl Yastrzemski never hit 50 HR's in a season. Discounting 1922, when he hit 35 HR's playing in only 110 games because of suspensions, and 1925 when he hit 25 HR's playing in only 98 games because of an intestinal abscess, his average from 1920-1931 was 50.4. He hit .393 in 1923, and was a lifetime .342 hitter. His slugging percentage in 1920 was .846 and his lifetime slugging average was .692 — both records.

• • •

Walter Johnson's career strikeout total was eclipsed by Steve Carlton and Nolan Ryan. Another of his records will not likely be broken. What is this record?

His 113 shutouts. Johnson's 416 career wins is well short of Cy Young's 511, but it should be noted that 10 times his Washington Senators finished in the second division. Three times he won 25 games with clubs that finished seventh. He also holds the hit-batsmen record at 206. Don Drysdale is second with 154.

• • •

Arnold Rothstein's name will go down in baseball

history although he never even played a minute of pro ball. Do you know why?

He was the man who paid eight Chicago White Sox players to throw the 1919 World Series. The eight accomplices, Ed Cicotte, Claude Williams, Oscar Felsch, Joe Jackson, Charles Risberg, Fred McMullin, Buck Weaver and Chick Gandil, were all expelled from baseball for life. The scandal also kept Jackson and Weaver out of the Hall of Fame.

• • •

Babe Ruth and Ty Cobb both said they admired this man's swing enough to watch him when they were in a slump. Who is he?

Shoeless Joe Jackson, third on the all-time batting average list with .356.

• • •

Ty Cobb's batting was peculiar for a reason other than his high average. What was it?

He batted with his hands apart. His bottom hand was on the end of the bat, his top hand a few inches up the handle. He adjusted his hand to the pitcher he was facing. He would keep his hands apart for the better pitchers, content to rap a single. Against lesser pitchers, he would slide his top hand down to hit with more power. His results are worth noting. He hit .300 or better for 23 straight years, achieving .400 three times. He won twelve batting titles, nine in a row. He achieved a triple crown in 1909. He has the highest lifetime batting average at .367. Only Ted Williams (on two occasions), Rod Carew and George Brett have hit that high in any one season. Don't forget his 4191 hits, either.

• • •

Cobb's hitting was such that it overshadowed his other specialty, which was . . .

. . . base stealing. His 96 stolen bases was an AL record for

67 years, and his 892 career stolen bases is still the AL record. For 12 straight seasons he stole 30 or more bases. Nine times he stole 40 or more, eight times he stole 50 or more, six times he stole 60 or more and between 1909-1912 he averaged 71 SB's.

• • •

The Phillies played for many years in an unusual ball park. Can you remember it?
Baker Bowl was built in 1887, and the Phillies somehow played in it until 1938. Clubhouse attendant Ted Kessler remembered it as a firetrap in his days there as a batboy and fireman.

"After the ball game, firemen would come in and put out the burning cigarettes. They had barrels of water all over the park and buckets of water, too, hanging on nails. If I or anyone saw a fire — there were lots of fires — we would take a bucket off the wall and douse the fire."

The Bowl accommodated a mere fifteen thousand fans, but after 1933, it averaged 2,000 people per game. The right field wall was only 280 feet from the plate. Babe Herman called hitting there "a pleasure." One curve ball he hit over the screen "went across two sidewalks to the old railroad station. It went with the wind at least 550 feet. A kid brought it back in." In 1930, the Phillies as a whole hit .315, but only won 52 games. They finished dead last, 40 games back, with a team ERA of 6.71. The Phils led the league in errors and allowed an average of eight runs, earned and unearned, a game.

This kind of disastrous ball resulted in a fan scrawling on a stadium ad for Lifebuoy soap: "The Phillies use Lifebuoy and they still stink."

• • •

Song-and-dance man Benny Fields played a little game involving baseball. What was it?
He would challenge people to name an all-star team con-

sisting of major league players whose nicknames were the names of animals and insects.

His team consisted of: Rabbit Maranville, Moose McCormick, Ox Eckhardt, Flea Clifton, Spider Jorgensen, Harry (The Cat) Brecheen, Goose Goslin, Ducky Medwick and Hippo Jim Vaughn. He also included lesser lights Turkey Tyson, Mule Haas and Bullfrog Dietrich.

The tradition of an animal nickname has continued to the present. Today one could field a team including Mark "The Bird" Fidrych, Goose Gossage, Hawk Dawson, Gorman "Perching Bird" Thomas, Moose Skowron, Jim "Bulldog" Bouton, Catfish Hunter, Mudcat Grant, Dave "Cobra" Parker, Kent "Stork" Tekulve and "Bull" Luzinski.

● ● ●

How did Hall-of-Fame umpire "Honest" John Kelly get his nickname?

Kelly, who umpired in the National League, was once riding to Akron by horse with a friend over wintry roads, when the horse bolted into a snowdrift. Kelly and his friend escaped injury by jumping from the wagon, and walked three miles to a farmhouse.

There they were greeted at the door by a bewhiskered old man holding a lantern.

"My name is John Kelly, and I want to hire a conveyance to get to town," the umpire said.

"I ain't never heard of ye, but ye look honest to me, John Kelly, and I'll give ye a lift," the farmer said.

Kelly gave the farmer two dollars and promised to return the rig the next day. When he reached Akron, the horse died. The next day Kelly returned to the farmhouse on his stylish buggy with the farmer's buckboard in tow. The farmer's face fell when he saw the mare was missing, but Kelly explained the circumstances, and paid the farmer twenty dollars for a replacement. "You're honest,

John Kelly," the farmer said, and the nickname, an excellent one for an umpire, stuck.

• • •

How did an uncaught foul ruin the 1912 World Series for the New York Giants?

Contrary to popular belief, the decisive play of the 1912 World Series was not Fred Snodgrass' famous $30,000 muff (Snodgrass dropped an easy fly ball), but, rather, a Keystone Kops routine by the New York Giants' best players.

With runners on first and second *after* Snodgrass' muff, Tris Speaker was up. He lifted a high foul on the right side, and no one broke for it. Finally, catcher Chief Meyers took off, and Fred Merkle came in from first. Speaker expected Merkle to get it, but to his amazement, pitcher Christy Mathewson was calling Merkle off the ball and Meyers onto it — while Merkle was practically under the ball. Merkle backed off, Mathewson and Meyers came in — and the ball dropped in the triangle the three Giants formed.

As they went back to their positions, Speaker said to Mathewson, "Matty, that will cost you the Series."

On the next pitch, Speaker ripped a single, which tied the game, and then Larry Gardner hit a long fly that brought home the winning run. Tris Speaker called the single off Matty his biggest moment in the majors.

The supreme irony of the incident was that the three Giants were Manager John McGraw's smartest, most alert players.

• • •

The Excelsior baseball club of Brooklyn, 1860, laid down the law to ball players who argued with the ump. Can you recall how they did it?

To quote from the Constitution of the Brooklyn Excelsiors, Rule 9: "Members, when assembled for field practice, or for any meeting of the club, who shall use profane or improper language, shall be fined ten cents for each offense." Rule 10 stated that "a member disputing the decisions of the umpire shall be fined twenty-five cents for each offense." Rule 11 warned that "a member who shall audibly express his opinion on a doubtful play before the decision of the umpire (unless called upon to do so) shall be fined twenty-five cents for each offense." The fines were to be paid to the ump on leaving the field.

* * *

Fernando Valenzuela won the 1981 Cy Young Award. But who had the best record of any starting pitcher in the Majors?

In 1981, in a strike-shortened season, Fernando Valenzuela salvaged the otherwise dismal year with his considerable pitching feats. Among his achievements was leading the National League in starts with 25, in complete games with 11, strikeouts with 180, and shutouts with 8. But the chubby right-handed Mexican's 13-7 record was not the best in the National League.

Tom Seaver, with the Cincinnati Reds, notched a brilliant 14-2 record, leading in wins and winning percentage (.875).

But Valenzuela, who drew huge crowds, and electrified Latin-American fans, prevented Seaver from winning what would have been his fourth Cy Young Award.

* * *

How did a skunk help win a game?

It's hard to believe that a Hoosier skunk helped win a baseball game, but that is, in fact, what happened at Patoka Park in Hazelton, Indiana, back in 1908.

Evansville was ahead in the sixth inning, when one of the Patoka boys slammed the ball into the right field. The Evansville outfielder saw the ball sail into the cornfield and headed in that direction to retrieve it. He soon emerged from between the cornstalks holding the ball as far away from himself as possible. The Patoka boy's fly ball had konked a skunk ambling through the cornfield. The skunk, of course, returned fire, releasing its highly malodorous spray all over the area.

The remainder of the game progressed poorly for Evansville as the wind continued to blow from the cornfield and across the baseball diamond. The Evansville boys, unused to this sort of treatment, did not handle the situation well. Three of them got sick, allowing Patoka to come up from behind, winning the game, 7-6.

• • •

On June 10, 1897, a baseball game took place at Princeton University in which no one pitched. Do you remember the reason for this unusual occurrence?

This particular game was attended by many professors at Princeton as well as distinguished guests such as Mrs. Grover Cleveland. The reason so many people attended the game was that a pitching machine, instead of a pitcher, was playing the game.

Professor C.H. Hinton, an instructor in mathematics at Princeton, invented the pitching machine that stood on the mound that day. Since the machine took so much time between pitches, the game ended after three full innings. Nevertheless, its record for the day was not bad: 8 strikeouts, 1 wild pitch, 1 base on balls and 4 hits.

At the beginning of the game, batters were somewhat fearful of the machine and often jumped away from the curve ball pitches. When the machine began to throw several into the strike zone, however, the batters mustered their courage and stood closer to the plate.

It is not known what became of the pitching machine after its debut at Princeton University. Very possibly, the professor grew weary of trying to improve it, teach it new techniques or encourage it to chew tobacco. And, of course, it could not talk to the press!

• • •

Two of the American League's top hitters of 1945 were released the following year. Who were they?

The fates were not kind to the White Sox' Tony "Cooch" Cuccinello and John "Ugly" Dickshot. Cuccinello hit .308 and Dickshot hit .302, making them second and third, respectively, in the American League batting race. But both were handed their walking papers in 1946.

Cuccinello was a veteran who saw more playing time in that 1945 season because the White Sox' real stars were in the army, fighting World War II. In a 15-year career with the Reds, Giants, Dodgers, Braves and White Sox, he amassed a .280 lifetime average and hit more than .300 five times as a regular.

Dickshot didn't last as long as Cuccinello. He played a few games from 1936 to 1938 for the Pittsburgh Pirates and was with the Giants in 1939. The White Sox brought him out of obscurity in 1944 and in 1945 he had his best and final season.

The batting king that season in the American League was George "Snuffy" Stirnweiss, who hit .309, with ten home runs. His average then plummeted in 1946 to .251 and although he did not get his walking papers, he would only hit ten more home runs over the next seven *years*.

• • •

The World Series of 1920 set three records. Do you remember them?

By the fifth game, the two teams were tied at two games apiece. Both managers were starting star pitchers: Burleigh Grimes for Brooklyn and Jim Bagby for Cleveland. From the very first inning, Grimes was having trouble. The first two Indian batters reached base on singles. When Tris Speaker, the Indians' playing manager, bunted,

Grimes tried to field it and fell flat on his back. Elmer Smith came to bat with the bases loaded. Smith's record for 1920 was .316. The first two pitches were strikes, the third a ball, and then Grimes shot a fast ball toward the plate. It was just what Smith had been anticipating. He hit the ball to right field where it disappeared behind the screen. It was the first grand slam home run in World Series history. Thirty-three years later, a second grand slam was hit by Mickey Mantle of the Yanks in the 1953 Series against the Dodgers.

In the fourth inning, the Tribe's Doc Johnston got a single, stole second and went to third on an infield out. Steve O'Neill was intentionally walked. Pitcher Bagby was up next and Grimes figured he could handle this weak hitter. He could not have been more wrong! Bagby slammed a line drive into the bleachers behind center field, scoring three more runs for the Indians. It was the first home run ever hit by a pitcher in a World Series.

By the fifth stanza, Grimes was out of the game. The Indians had thoroughly flattened him — seven runs in nine hits, including the two home runs. Bagby eased up a little in the fifth. Pete Kilduff and Otto Miller, the first two Dodger batters, singled, bringing up Grimes' replacement, Clarence Mitchell. Dodger manager Robinson decided to let his pitcher bat, instead of calling for a pinch hitter. He flashed the hit-and-run sign to Kilduff and Miller at first and second, indicating that they should run on the pitch. Mitchell met the ball nicely for what appeared to be a solid base hit. Bill Wambsganss, the Indian second baseman, hurled himself toward second base to cover the play, gave a dying leap for Mitchell's line drive, and caught it for one out. Kilduff, who had been on second, was now running to third. Wambsganss stepped on second base to hail Kilduff as out number two. Miller had been on first base, but was now nearing second. Realizing what had happened, he stopped, but it was too late. Wambsganss tagged him for the third out. This move completed the first and only unassisted triple play in World Series history.

When Mitchell came to bat for a second time, he hit right into a double play — executed by who other than Wambsganss. In only two at bats, Mitchell had hit into five outs.

The stunned Dodgers fell 8-1, although they outhit the Indians 13-12. The Tribe then shut them out the next two games, winning the Series.

• • •

Bobby Cox has managed teams other than the Toronto Blue Jays. Can you name any of them?
In addition to handling the Blue Jays, Cox has managed Fort Lauderdale (Florida State League), West Haven (Eastern League), Syracuse (International League), Atlanta (National League) and, in 1977, was a coach with the New York Yankees. A third baseman, Cox also played for the Yankees in 1968 and 1969.

• • •

Who was the Montreal Expos' player of the year in 1982?
Otherwise known as "Mr. Scoop," Al Oliver led the National League in batting with a .331 average, not to mention 109 runs batted in, 204 hits and 43 doubles. Oliver also hit 22 home runs and only struck out 61 times in 160 games.

This came as no surprise to those who have followed Oliver's career, starting in the majors with the Pittsburgh Pirates in 1968. Among other feats, Oliver hit three home runs in a game on May 23, 1979 and repeated the script on August 17, 1980.

In December 1977, Oliver was traded from the Pirates to the Texas Rangers. On March 31, 1982 he was dealt from Texas to the Montreal Expos.

Oliver's one World Series appearance was a disappointment. In 1971 he played in five series games for Pittsburgh and batted a puny .211, with four hits in 19 at-bats.

* * *

A baseball player was shot in the leg while in the army, but returned to pitch in the major leagues. Can you name him?

At the outbreak of World War II, Lou Brissie played baseball for his college team. Eric McNair, his coach and former Philadelphia Athletic shortstop, brought him down to see Connie Mack. Mack was impressed with Brissie, but did not want to take him right away. Mack advised Brissie to go to college first and then return to Philadelphia. He added that there would be a uniform waiting for him. Mack even helped Brissie with college expenses to show the young man how serious he was about the boy's future. Brissie, in turn, was determined to keep Mack's faith in him and continued playing in college.

A year after the bombing of Pearl Harbour, Brissie felt he could no longer put off enlisting. He told his college coach of his decision. McNair did not try to dissuade the boy. He knew the boy was strong willed and his efforts would be in vain.

Two years later, on December 7, 1944, Corporal Brissie and his infantry were in the Appenine Mountains outside of Bologna, Italy. German attackers shelled his platoon. Brissie and his entire outfit were hit. Most of the men were killed, the others critically wounded. Brissie was one of the more fortunate; nevertheless, he was badly wounded. He lay in mud until a search party arrived. To Brissie's dismay, they appeared to be leaving him there, assuming that all of the men had been killed. Brissie tried to call out to them but could not, due to shock. Then one of the men in the search party noticed Brissie move. Brissie was given medical attention at a nearby aid station. Forty transfusions later, Brissie was transferred to the evacuation hospital in Naples.

158

One morning, Brissie awoke to find a doctor leaning over him. The doctor turned to an aide and said, "This leg will have to come off." Brissie was stunned. He mustered all the strength he could and pleaded with the doctor not to amputate his leg. "I'm a baseball player, and I've got to play ball," Brissie explained. Fortunately for Brissie, the doctor was a baseball fan, and understood Brissie's plight. The boy's strong will to keep his leg encouraged the doctor to agree that he would do everything he could to save it for him.

Brissie's leg had been completely shattered. There was scarcely a piece of bone in his leg that was left intact. The doctor did everything he could to put Brissie's leg back together. Brissie underwent many complicated operations at various hospitals around the country and around the world.

Connie Mack had written Brissie through his years in the army, and after the boy was shot, wrote him more often. Connie assured Lou that there would still be a uniform waiting for him upon his release from the army.

One morning in July of 1946, Lou Brissie walked up to Connie Mack's office on a crutch. Just as Connie had promised, Lou's uniform was ready for him. Brissie wore the uniform and even warmed up with the bull-pen catcher. But the idea that he would ever play major league baseball still seemed far-fetched. Brissie underwent major surgery a few days later for an infection in his leg. Most of the Athletics thought they had seen the last of Lou Brissie.

Lou Brissie showed up at spring training in Florida the next year, much to the surprise of the other players. Although not as agile as most, Brissie still managed to play ball. Only one year later, Brissie was pitching for the Philadelphia Athletics. By the end of his career Brissie had pitched six full seasons of major league ball.

• • •

Name the player who stole home without knowing it.

Fred Clarke, the player-manager of the 1906 Pittsburgh Pirates, was on third with the bases loaded against the Cubs. The count on the batter was 3-1 when the Chicago pitcher wound up and threw what appeared to be a shoulder-high ball four. When the umpire did not immediately signal physically or verbally, Clarke assumed the pitch had, indeed, been called a ball, walking the batter and forcing him across home plate.

Clarke was obviously not the only one who thought that way. The batter heard nothing to disprove this notion, so he dropped his bat and began to walk down to first base. Now the catcher was convinced also, and threw the ball back to the pitcher. In the meantime, Clarke ambled toward the plate and as he crossed into the batter's box, was greeted by an extremely slow strike call by the umpire.

Jaws dropped and all eyes swiveled to the man in blue. "Frog in my throat," the embarrassed official said. "Couldn't get a word out." The batter returned to finish his at-bat, but since time had never been called, Clarke's run — and steal — counted.

* * *

Which pitcher had the greatest success against Babe Ruth?

It is an oddity that the man who struck out the great Babe an amazing 19 out of 23 times they faced each other could not find the same formula against the rest of the American League. Hub Pruett, in his seven years in the majors, had a 29-48 record, with an ERA of 4.63, while pitching for the St. Louis Browns, Philadelphia Phillies, New York Giants and Boston Braves.

* * *

Which player with an artificial limb became a major league pitcher for a day?

Bert Shepard of the Washington Senators.

In March of 1945, Shepard walked up to the pre-season training camp of the Washington Senators at College Park, Maryland. He wanted to speak with Manager Ossie Bluege.

Bert asked to try out for the Senators. He offered Bluege his credentials: Wisconsin State League, Evangeline League and the Arizona-Texas League. He had pitched and played while in the Army, as well. Since good baseball players were so scarce during the war (almost all physically fit men were drafted), Bluege didn't want to turn down an able body. He gave Shepard a uniform and told him he could try out.

When Shepard was in the locker room changing, the other players didn't take much notice of him at first, since there were often people who tried out and were never seen again. Then they noticed that Shepard had an artificial leg. When he walked onto the field, his limp was somewhat noticeable, but probably more so because the other players knew he only had one leg. Shepard had lost his leg in the war.

Shepard wanted to pitch, but wasn't afforded the opportunity. Bluege used him mostly for batting practice. One day in July of 1945, Shepard finally got his chance to pitch. The Senators were playing the Dodgers in exhibition. Bert knew this was probably his only chance to pitch against major league opposition. He pitched the game and won.

In July Shepard had another chance to pitch. He was put in as a relief pitcher against the Red Sox. In five innings he held the Red Sox to three hits and one run. He struck out three batters.

Shepard's career in the major leagues was certainly short, but inspirational, nonetheless, for other war veterans. The injury and loss he had suffered in the war could not keep Bert Shepard from realizing his life's ambition, even if only for a couple of games.

• • •

161

9

1. Who is the all-time leader in career saves?
2. Who is the all-time leader in shutouts pitched?
3. Name the only two players of this century to have an ERA of under two runs scored per game for their career.
4. Babe Ruth is the career leader in base on balls. Where does Hank Aaron rank among career "walkers"?
5. What pitcher appeared in the most games in one season and what is the number of games he was in?
6. Who holds the record for most losses in one season in 20th-century baseball?
7. Who holds the record for most RBI's in one season and in what year did he do it?
8. Has anyone ever pitched a no-hitter and lost?
9. Who won the Rookie of the Year Awards in both leagues in 1965?
10. Who was the on-deck batter when Bobby Thomson hit the "shot heard 'round the world" in the 1951 play-off?

Answers begin on page 172.

Which two teams played the first game ever in the United States, with playing rules and guidelines?
The New York Nine and the New Jersey Knickerbockers were the first two *amateur* teams to play under rules — on June 19, 1846, at Elysian Fields in Hoboken, New Jersey. Alexander J. Cartwright, who established the rules, umpired the Nine's 23-1 victory. It is believed that this game led to the formation of organized baseball in the United States.

• • •

Which pitcher was the victim of Babe Ruth's first major league home run?
Jack Warhop, who at this time — 1915 — was at the tag end of an eight-year career with the New York Yankees. He amassed a 68-94 lifetime record, with a 3.09 ERA.

• • •

Which pitcher lost the first New York Met game?
Roger Craig received the losing decision for the Mets at Busch Stadium on April 11, 1962.

• • •

Which team was first to play baseball professionally?
In 1869 the city of Cincinnati paid its players, in an attempt to rid the team of its losing ways. Harry Wright, a jeweler and ex-cricketer, was hired for $12,000 to manage the Red Stockings. The club then won 56 of their next 57 games. Unfortunately they rediscovered their losing ways and were soon forced to fold because of increasing salaries!

• • •

How and when did shoe polish salvage a World Series?
1957 was the first year of World Series play for the Braves since moving from Boston. The first two games were played in New York, with the Yanks winning the first and

the Braves winning the second contest. The two teams then travelled to an overjoyed Milwaukee where Wisconsin fans awaited their very first Series.

Some of the high enthusiasm died down when the Braves' pitchers walked eleven Yanks and lost the first home game, 12-3. The next day Braves' pitcher Warren Spahn, the great southpaw, took the mound for the fourth game of the Series. Eight innings later, the veteran had the Yankees down, 4-1. Spahn retired the first two batters in the ninth and then faced Yogi Berra. Yogi singled and so did Gil McDougald right after him.

Manager Fred Haney held a conference on the mound with Spahn, assuring the pitcher of his confidence in him. Elston Howard, the next Yankee at bat, stepped up to the batter's box and the count quickly reached three and two. Spahn's next pitch hit Howard's bat with a crack and sailed out of the park for a sure home run. The score was now tied. Milwaukee failed to score in the bottom of the ninth.

The tenth inning began with the Yankees' Hank Bauer batting in Tony Kubek; the Braves were now down 5-4. Nippy Jones was sent in to bat for Spahn in the bottom of the tenth.

Jones slowly walked up to the plate, tapped the dirt off his spikes, and got ready for the pitch. Tommy Byrne, the Yanks' relief pitcher, let go of the pitch, a ball. Catcher Berra failed to get a handle on it and it skidded back to the grandstand wall. Jones began to walk to first, but was called back by the umpire.

A healthy argument erupted as Jones claimed he had been hit in the foot by the low pitch. Umpire Angie Donatelli called the pitch a ball and ordered Jones back to the plate. Meanwhile the wayward ball had rolled back from the wall and came to rest between Jones and Donatelli. Jones picked up the ball and thrust it in the umpire's face.

"Here!" Jones exclaimed. "Look at the shoe polish on the ball." That was all Nippy had to say. Donatelli took one look at the black mark on the ball and awarded the batter first base. A pinch-runner was set in.

The bizarre event seemed to awaken the Braves' hitters. Milwaukee shortstop Johnny Logan doubled, driving in the pinch runner, and the score was again tied. Eddie Mathews, the Braves' third baseman, stepped up to the plate and cracked out a home run, scoring Logan ahead of him. The Braves won the game, 7-5.

Milwaukee had beaten the Yanks and tied the Series at two games apiece. Heightened by their victory, they played their way to further victories in seven games. But their tremendous victory might never have happened were it not for Nippy Jones and his well-shined shoes.

• • •

Which pitcher called in his infielders and outfielders to watch him strike out the side in the ninth inning?
Rube Waddell, when pitching for the Philadelphia Athletics between 1902 and 1907, reportedly did this on more than one occasion. Fans claimed they had seen the fielders sitting on the grass idly watching Waddell strike out the side. However, manager Connie Mack adamantly denied that Waddell had ever done it in a "real" ball game. What do you suppose Mack thought a "real" ball game was?

• • •

Who batted in twelve runs for the St. Louis Cardinals during one game?
"Sunny" Jim Bottomley slugged in twelve runs for the Cards against the Brooklyn Dodgers on September 16, 1924 at Ebbets Field. The Dodgers were caught up in a tight race for the pennant, while the Cardinals were slipping in sixth place. This was a defeat Brooklyn did not need.

Bottomley got six hits, including two home runs, a double, and three singles. The Cards won the game, 17-3. The display was especially disheartening for Wilbert Robinson, the Dodger manager, since Bottomley's feat broke a record Robinson set in 1892 — eleven runs with a seven-for-seven performance.

Anger was instrumental in Bottomley's success. When he came to the fourth inning, Jim had already driven in three runs. Men were on second and third when "Uncle Robbie" called for an intentional pass to Rogers Hornsby (who was having his most successful season). Furious at this show of contempt, Bottomley determined to redress the slight. He sent a homer over the right field wall with the bases loaded, bringing his RBI total for the game to seven.

In the sixth Bottomley hit another over the right field wall, bringing in two more runs. A single in the seventh brought in two more, and another single in the ninth garnered his twelfth RBI.

• • •

Name the team that played two complete World Series without using a single substitute.
Through Manager Connie Mack's astute stewardship, the Philadelphia Athletics played the entire 1910 and 1913 World Series without a single substitution of players, including pitchers. Only two hurlers, Chief Bender and Jack Coombs, appeared for the A's in the 1910 Fall Classic, and three in 1913 — Bender, Eddie Plank and Bullet Joe Bush. Using his fixed lineup, Mack's Athletics won both Series, four games to one — the first against the Cubs and the second against the Giants.

• • •

Who was the first American League pitcher to throw two no-hitters in one season?
Allie Reynolds of the New York Yankees pitched two no-hit games in 1951. One was against the Cleveland Indians, on July 12; and the other was against the Boston Red Sox

on September 28. The part-Cree Indian ball player was known as Manager Casey Stengel's clutch pitcher. He was also known as a very cool-headed hurler. Against the Indians he broke a baseball tradition by mentioning the words "no-hitter" to his teammates. According to the superstition, if these words were uttered during the course of a game, the performance was sure to be ruined. Fortunately for the New York Yankees, Reynolds was not superstitious.

• • •

Who holds the consecutive hit record for a pitcher?

Don Larsen of the St. Louis Browns connected on seven straight hits as a pitcher in 1953. Unfortunately he wasn't as successful on the mound as he was at the plate. Aside from his fabled 1956 perfect game, he was only 81-91 over 14 years, with a 3.78 ERA in the majors.

• • •

Which city has had its team(s) represented as "cellar-dwellers" the greatest number of times?

Despite the recent public relations slogan, "Philadelphia, The City of Champions," Philadelphians have been treated to a grand total of 44 last-place baseball clubs. The American League Philadelphia Athletics landed in the cellar 19 times before their demise in 1955. The Phillies, in spite of their recent success, hit rock bottom a total of 25 times!

They didn't do it by themselves. The Phillies operated in the 1930s as a farm team, training ball players for the bigs until they could be sold for more money. And the Phillies fell into another streak of hard times in the 1960s, when they lost 21 games in a row one year — and their pitching staff was one of the worst ever in the majors.

The Athletics had a strong team until 1915, when owner Connie Mack broke it up, fearing that the new Federal League would grab his players. He reasoned that he would make money from them before they could jump their contracts and go to the new league. The team, now minus most of its stars after Mack later reassembled it, dwelt in the cellar for many years.

By 1931 the rejuvenated A's had won three straight pennants. But Mack, deep in Depression financial woes, couldn't afford to pay his players. Consequently he sold the team again, and the A's did not win another pennant in Philadelphia.

• • •

Why didn't Babe Ruth, Ty Cobb, Honus Wagner or Hack Wilson ever win the MVP award?
The award wasn't created until 1931. From 1911 to 1930 the outstanding player in each league was honored with the Chalmers Award, given out in conjunction with the Chalmers automobile. The AL award also had the provision that there would be no repeat winners. In 1927 when Babe Ruth hit 60 homers, Lou Gehrig won the award, as Ruth was a past recipient.

• • •

1930 was called the Year of the Hitter. Hack Wilson set the major league record of 190 RBI's and Bill Terry became the last National Leaguer to hit over .400. 1968 was called the Year of the Pitcher. Two outstanding pitchers set four records. What were the records and who set them?
Bob Gibson set an ERA record (for pitchers with 300 innings pitched) with a 1.12 ERA and a league-leading 268 strikeouts. The other pitcher was Don Drysdale, who set records of six straight shut-outs and 58 2/3 consecutive scoreless innings.

Drysdale was also the beneficiary of an unusual call by an umpire. On May 31, bases loaded, no outs, ninth inning, Drysdale hit Dick Dietz with a pitch, but umpire Harry Wedelstedt ruled that Dietz had not made a reasonable effort to avoid the pitch. It was called a ball. Dietz then popped to short left and the runner couldn't tag up. Drysdale retired the next two batters to end the game.

* * *

Jack Chesbro holds the post-1900 record for pitching wins in one season with 41. He pitched for a New York team. What team was it?

They were the New York Highlanders, later known as the Yankees. 1904 was a phenomenal season for Chesbro. His statistics were as follows: 41-13, completing his first 30 games and 48 of 55 that year, winning 14 games in succession. He pitched 454 2/3 innings, almost a third of the NY staff's total. He led the league in ERA with 1.82; games won, 41; percentage, .774; games pitched, 55; games started, complete games, and innings pitched.

Ed Walsh of the Chicago White Sox had nearly as good a season four years later. His statistics were almost as mind boggling — 40 wins, 49 starts, 42 complete games, 464 innings pitched, 269 strikeouts, and 12 shutouts. He walked but 56 and had seven saves. Incidentally, in 1907, Jack Chesbro had the honor of giving up the first major league hit to Ty Cobb.

* * *

Which major-league manager once called for a pinch-hitter who hadn't been on the roster for two years?

Leo "The Lip" Durocher. Late in a game in which the Chicago Cubs were trailing by one run, Chicago manager Leo Durocher barked: "Tell Willie Smith to get ready, I'm going to pinch-hit with him." A pregnant silence fell over the Cubs' dugout. Finally, Jim Hickman, who had always had a fondness for Durocher, clambered from his seat at the other end of the bench, strode over to Durocher and, in quiet tones, asserted: "Skip! Willie Smith hasn't been with

169

us for two years. But if you really want me to, I'll find him and bring him back."

• • •

Novelist Ernest Hemingway was knocked out in a boxing match with a big-league pitcher. Who was the hurler and how did he manage to outfight the author?
Brooklyn Dodgers' superb relief pitcher Hugh Casey did the drum roll on Ernest Hemingway's head in 1941. The episode all came about when Dodgers' boss Larry Mac-Phail decided to take his Brooklyns to Havana, Cuba, for spring training. It turned out that Hemingway, who dominated American literature, was living in Cuba at the time. A galvanic sports fan, Hemingway also fancied himself a boxer and occasionally would invite his guests to go a round or two with him.

On this occasion Dodgers' broadcaster Red Barber had accompanied Casey to Hemingway's house. According to Barber, Hemingway looked Casey over and figured he could outpunch the pitcher. "Casey looked so innocent," Barber remembered. "He was a big man with a large stomach. He had rosey apple cheeks and spoke softly in his Georgia accent."

Once Casey and Barber entered the author's house, Hemingway pulled out a set of boxing gloves. Casey later told friends what followed:

"Hemingway insisted I put on the gloves and spar with him. I didn't want to box with him. After all, when I was a little younger I'd done some fighting.

"But Hemingway wouldn't let me alone. Finally, I put on the gloves, and he said he'd just fool around. Before I knew it he was belting me as hard as he could. I told him to cut it out. He hit me harder than ever."

Hemingway, who thought he had calculated adroitly when first challenging Casey, committed two key *faux pas*. He didn't realize that Casey was once a fair-to-middlin' fighter; and he underestimated the pitcher's burning pride.

"On the surface," said Barber, "Casey looked like a mild man, but he was a rough one."

Too late, Hemingway made this discovery. After the author tagged the pitcher one time too many, Casey struck his host.

"I just knocked him down," Casey concluded, "and that ended boxing for the night."

• • •

Which ballpark boasted the most difficult "hit sign, win suit" sign in the major leagues?

Ebbets Field, Brooklyn. Home of the Dodgers, Ebbets Field had a massive scoreboard located in right center-field. At the base of the scoreboard, a long, thin billboard, measuring approximately four feet high by 40 feet wide, proclaimed the advantages of shopping at Abe Stark's clothing shop on Pitkin Avenue in the East New York section of Brooklyn. In one corner of the billboard an invitation to batters proclaimed: "HIT SIGN, WIN SUIT!" Stark sold suits and gladly would award one to any batter who wacked a ball off the sign. The only problem was that the sign was so situated that it was virtually impossible to hit with a line drive — the sign was too close to the ground. Besides, it was equally difficult to hit with a high fly ball, because they were usually flagged down by either the right or centerfielder. The sign was later immortalized in *The New Yorker* magazine — except in the magazine cartoon it was moved to left field and Stark was drawn in, sitting in the front row with a baseball glove in his hand, leaning over to catch the ball before it hit the sign.

• • •

ANSWERS

QUICKIE QUIZ 1

1. He hit exactly 56 singles and scored 56 runs. **2.** Because the distance from the pitching rubber to home plate was 50 feet, 45 feet prior to 1876. **3.** '87-5, '85-7, '84-6, '81-7, '80-8, '79-9. **4.** A man advancing on another player's hit was credited with a stolen base. **5.** Walks counted as hits. **6.** New York Highlander pitcher Jack Chesbro won 41 games in 1904. **7.** Answers to A, B, C and D are the same player — Babe Ruth. **8.** The Father of *Modern* Baseball. **9.** 216. **10.** Mickey Mantle, Joe DiMaggio, Jimmie Foxx, Stan Musial, Yogi Berra and Roy Campanella.

QUICKIE QUIZ 2

1. Rogers Hornsby and Ted Williams. **2.** Nap Lajoie — .422 — 13 HR's — 125 RBI's. **3.** Jackie Robinson. **4.** Five. Five HR's in one series, three consecutive HR's in a game, four HR's in consecutive official AB's over two games, 25 total bases, and 10 runs. **5.** The 1892 Boston Beaneaters went 102-48. **6.** The 1878 Boston Beaneaters won the pennant with a 41-19 record. **7.** The L.A. Dodgers won the 1981 pennant with 63 wins. **8.** In 1902, Pittsburgh ended the season winning 103 games. Brooklyn was "right" behind with only 75 games. **9.** In 1962 Tom Cheney struck out 21 batters in a 16-inning game. **10.** John Burnette had nine hits in an extra-innings game in 1932.

QUICKIE QUIZ 3

1. Rogers Hornsby, .358. **2.** Babe Ruth, 1356. **3.** Ruth and Gehrig, 61 and 46 for 108. **4.** Gehrig with 184, an AL record. **5.** Harmon Killebrew. **6.** Lefty O'Doul with 334. O'Doul is also second (with Bill Terry) in hits in one season with 254.

George Sisler clinched the record with 257. **7.** Warren Spahn with the NL record of 35. **8.** It was really Joe's *second* longest professional hitting streak. He batted safely in 61 consecutively AB's in 1933 in the PCL. **9.** The pitch Ruth hit was on a 2-2 count (second ball, second strike). It was also the Babe's second HR of the game, which was followed on the next pitch by Gehrig's second homer of the game.

QUICKIE QUIZ 4

1 - c, **2** - e, **3** - b, **4** - a, **5** - d, **6** - g, **7** - f, **8** - h, **9** - i, **10** - j.

QUICKIE QUIZ 5

1. The "Perfesser," Casey Stengel. The 1962 Mets were so adept at losing games (120 lost and 60 1/2 games out of first place) that their winning percentage calculated to .250. Among the many notable players on the team were Choo-Choo Coleman and Marvelous Marv Throneberry, whose build and stance in the batter's box resembled Mickey Mantle, yet was almost comical in skill. The quote was reputably uttered after watching Al Jackson pitch three-hit ball for 15 innings, only to lose on two errors committed by Marvelous Marv. **2.** Satchel Paige, a long-time star in the Negro league. Records were hard to verify when kept in these leagues, but some estimate his pitching for 30-40 years, winning over 2,000 games. In 1948, he joined major league baseball as a pitcher for the Cleveland Indians and listed his age as 42. **3.** Mel Allen, voice of the Yankees for years, is credited with this auctioneer-like cry to describe home runs in Yankee Stadium. **4.** Cuban-born Mike Gonzalez. As a scout with a not-too-commanding mastery of the English language, his report back to the parent club on a young minor league prospect who was fielding well but not hitting up to par was credited with telephoning this immortal phrase. **5.** Wee Willie Keeler. In 1897, Keeler's batting average at year's end was an outstanding .432. Responding to a reporter's query on how someone his size (5'4") could hit .432, Keeler revealed,"Simple. I keep my eyes clear and I hit 'em where they ain't." **6.** The words appear in a poem written by a man many believe to be among the greatest sports writers who ever lived, Grantland Rice. In comparing sports to life he wrote, "when the Great Scorer" comes to tally what you've done "it's not whether you win or lose, but how you play the game." **7.** Leo "The Lip" Durocher. While a coach with the Dodgers, Leo was asked why he liked one of his players, Ed Stanky (known as "the brat"). The Lip responded by explaining how Stanky always gave 100% and tried to give 125%. Then the Giants came out of the dugout led by Mel Ott. "Take a look at number four there, a nicer guy never drew a breath than that man there." The Lip then called off the names of the Giant players as they came out of the dugout. "Take a look at them. All nice guys. They'll finish last. Nice guys. Finish last." Although commonly written as one sentence, the quote is actually two. **8.** A little boy said it to Shoeless Joe Jackson in 1919 as Joe left the courtroom during the famous Black Sox scandal. The little boy asked him to "say it ain't so, Joe." "Yes, I'm afraid it is," Joe responded. Then the boy quipped, "I never would've thought it."

QUICKIE QUIZ 6

1. Seven times. **2.** Ken McKenzie, 5-4, 4.95, and Ray Daviault, 1-5, 6.22. **3.** Reggie Cleveland, then with Boston, in 1975. **4.** Russ Ford, who was 13-20, with a 3.35 ERA for the 1912 New York Yankees. **5.** Catcher Buck Martinez, who hit .229 with 4 homers in 72 games for the Royals. **6.** The Expos received Rich Coggins, Dave McNally and Bill Kirkpatrick. Coggins played only 13 games for Montreal, McNally retired, and Kirkpatrick never reached the bigs. Singleton and Torrez are still active. **7.** Karl Kuehl was named in early 1976, and he won 43 and lost 85 before being replaced by Charlie Fox. The Expos finished in the cellar. **8.** Jim Mason, who hit one off Pat Zachry of the Reds for the Yankees in the 1976 World Series, game 3. **9.** Robert L. Miller, who pitched for 14 teams from 1957 to 1974. **10.** Doug Ault, who is now the Jays' minor league hitting instructor.

QUICKIE QUIZ 7

1. The Jays defeated the White Sox, 9-5, on April 6, 1977. Bill Singer started for the Jays against Ken Brett. **2.** Pete Vuckovich won the game in relief, and won the 1982 Cy Young Award with the Milwaukee Brewers. **3.** George Selkirk, of Huntsville, Ontario, who replaced Babe Ruth in right field for the Yankees, and hung on there, hitting .290, for nine seasons. **4.** Phil Marchildon, from Penatanguishene, Ontario, lost 16 in 1946, and won 19 in 1947, both to lead the American League. His career was shortened by the injuries from his wartime sojourn in a German PoW camp. He had been an RCAF pilot. **5.** Doyle Alexander. The Jays acquired him in June 1983. **6.** George Gibson, who skippered the Pirates and Cubs in the 1920s. **7.** Fred Lake, from Nova Scotia. He ran the Red Sox in 1908 and 1909, and the Braves in 1910. **8.** Manny Mota, who only lasted 31 games with the Expos. **9.** Terry Puhl, from Melville, Saskatchewan. He hit .526 in the playoffs, but the Astros lost. **10.** Rusty Staub, who pinch-hit for the Mets with gusto, and pitcher Steve Renko, who won 6 games with the original Expos. He played for the Royals in 1983 and was released at season's end.

QUICKIE QUIZ 8

1. Zoilo Versalles, Minnesota, 1965. **2.** Although MVP's were selected beforehand, 1931 was the first year in which the Baseball Writers Association selected the winner. That year Frankie Frisch of the St. Louis Cardinals (NL) and Lefty

Grove from Philadelphia (AL) won. **3.** Jimmy Foxx of Philadelphia won in 1932 and 1933. Hal Newhouser from the
Detroit Tigers won in 1944 and '45. Mike Schmidt of the
Philadelphia Phillies won in 1980 and 1981. Joe Morgan of
the Reds won in 1975 and '76. The Cubs' Ernie Banks was
MVP in 1958 and 1959. The Braves' Dale Murphy won in
1982 and 1983. **4.** Allie Reynolds, who threw two no-hitters
in 1951. **5.** Vida Blue, Glen Abbott, Paul Lindblad and Rollie
Fingers no-hit the California Angels on September 28, 1975,
5-0. **6.** Mike McCormick of the San Francisco Giants won it
in the NL while Jim Lonborg won it in the AL. **7.** Bert
Blyleven, then playing for the Minnesota Twins, was a distant second with 258 K's in 1973. **8.** Lou Gehrig. **9.** Roy
Hartsfield. **10.** Brooks Robinson participated in 618 double
plays in his illustrious career.

QUICKIE QUIZ 9

1. Rollie Fingers, 272. **2.** Walter Johnson, 113. **3.** Ed
Walsh, 1.82 runs per game and Addie Joss, 1.88 runs per
game. **4.** He ranks 16th in all-time career walks with 1402.
5. Mike Marshall in 1974 appeared in 106 games. **6.** Vic
Willis lost 29 games in 1905. In 1906 he went 22-13. **7.** Hack
Wilson drove in 190 runs in 1930. **8.** Yes sir! In 1967, Steve
Barber and Stu Miller pitched a combined nine innings of
hitless ball and lost, 2-1. Ken Johnson of the Dodgers
pitched and lost a no-hitter, 1-0, April 23, 1964. **9.** Jim Lefeb-
vre won it in the National League and Curt Blefary won it in
the AL. They played for Los Angeles and Baltimore, respectively. **10.** None other than Willie Mays. One wonders what
would have happened if he had in fact gotten up.